Poems
That Speak
Words
about
Life

A Book of Poetry *with*
Christian Viewpoints

Amanda Libbers

WESTBOW
PRESS®
A DIVISION OF THOMAS NELSON
& ZONDERVAN

WestBow Press books may be ordered through booksellers or by contacting:

WestBow Press
A Division of Thomas Nelson & Zondervan
1663 Liberty Drive
Bloomington, IN 47403
www.westbowpress.com
1 (866) 928-1240

Scripture quotations taken from The Holy Bible, New International Version® NIV®
Copyright © 1973 1978 1984 2011 by Biblica, Inc. TM.
Used by permission. All rights reserved worldwide.

Scripture taken from the New King James Version® Copyright © 1982
by Thomas Nelson. Used by permission. All rights reserved.

ISBN: 978-1-9736-9401-4 (sc)
ISBN: 978-1-9736-9400-7 (hc)
ISBN: 978-1-9736-9444-1 (e)

Library of Congress Control Number: 2020911107

Print information available on the last page.

WestBow Press rev. date: 06/19/2020

About the Book

Poems that speak words about life highlight not only the good in life, but also the saddness of things that come people's way and the bad. When it highlights the bad their is saddness their and in saddness one is always able to turn a bad situation into a good one if they choose to do so. This is book filled with creative poetry some telling a story that illistrates Christian viewpoints and themes. Themes and scriptures built around creative unique poetry is cited at the end of each poem where it applies. Not all poetry involves the bible so not all poetry is cited, but all poems are united about some aspect of life or life experience either in a surreal way, a fantaical way, or in a literal sense.

May this book help those realize the good and the bad in life. May the good outshine the bad. May this book bless those who read it and help them gain wisdom and understanding about different aspects of life.

This book is dedicated primarily and firstly to Yahweh, Jesus Christ, and the Holy Spirit, and to those seeking a deeper knowledge of scripture.

This book is dedicated to David Libbers: Thank you for all of your hard work in assisting me with this project!

I would also like to dedicate this book to Father Chris Duncan of St. James Episcopal church in Baton Rouge, Louisiana for his assistance with locating scripture. Thank you, Father Chris Duncan!

I would like to dedicate and bless and honor my parents David and Elizabeth Libbers with this book! Thanks Elizabeth Libbers and David Libbers for seeing me through the good and the bad! Your support means so much to me and I can't thank you enough!

Preface

The poetry, which has Christian themes, has some information from scripture, is about scripture, is related to scripture, or is scripture used directly. If it is scripture directly used in the poem, it is referenced at the end of the poem. At the end of the poems, you may find content references. Content references are scriptures that are based on themes covered in that particular poem. Content references were not necessarily a particular scripture in mind used in the poem but simply cover themes and general topics that appear in the poem and are biblical. Content references were not inspirations for the poems themselves. They are for the reader's reference on those topics, and they support themes hidden within the poetry. Content reference scriptures is not quoted in any way within any of the poems and are more for the reader's knowledge on themes.

It is important to realize that not every poem uses scripture, but there may be an interpretation or opinion about scripture in general or specific parts of scripture. Not all poems have Christian themes, use scripture, or have an opinion or interpretation of scriptures used in themes, but non-Christian poems about life in this category follow what the Bible would say as the situation applies.

The Christian theme has scripture that has been interpreted and worded in my own unique style to fit the style of the poem. If scripture was not used directly within a given poem, then concepts from scripture based on interpretation may have been used. Although interpretation is arguable as to whether or not it is accurate, all interpretation in the poetry was done as literally as possible to follow scripture as closely as possible. There is absolutely no intent of deceit within the interpretation used based on scripture. I have tried to bring the interpretation of scripture, literally based, with some artistic creativity within the poem without changing the interpretation of scripture to be the literal interpretation. All interpretation of scripture is opinion of scripture in a literal sense.

Finally, it is important to know that artistic creativity was not used at all in interpretation of scripture in any way. Artistic creativity was used only in the poetry that surrounds the scripture or literal interpretation of scripture, which in some cases is an opinion of scripture. Not every poem needed a reference because it was creative in nature and did not include scripture or a theme from scripture. Most poems will contain a content reference, which is separate from a scripture reference. Scripture references are direct scripture used in the poems; content references are based on themes used in the poem. All poems, whether Christian based or not, are united in that they all deal with different aspects of "words about life" in a unique, poetic way.

Please enjoy *Poems That Speak Words about Life.*

Acknowledgments

I would like to especially thank David Libbers and Father Chris Duncan from St. James Episcopal Church in Baton Rouge, Louisiana, for their efforts in finding the locations of fourteen scriptures. After I described to them, the scripture was looked up in the One Touch Bible Soft Computer Program and inserted into the book. Thank you, David Libbers and Father Chris Duncan, for your assistance, efforts, and help in finding the name of the location of where these particular scriptures I asked about were located!

Note: **An example might be either Father Duncan or David Libbers giving a location, such as John 11:25–26, which I would have described to them. Then I would look up John 11:25–26 and quote the scripture in the manuscript using the One Touch Bible Soft Program. This was done for fourteen scriptures total. I located the rest of the scriptures in One Touch by myself.**

David Libbers is credited with finding most of the verses and looked first before Father Duncan was asked for help when needed. The verses they gave the locations for are as follows; all use the New International Version.

1. **Romans 10:9–13**
2. **Isaiah 58:11b**
3. **Luke 19:40**

4. Revelation 22:14
5. Revelation 22:17
6. 1 Corinthians 12:3
7. Matthew 18:19–20
8. John 14:16–18 (used twice)
9. John 8:11
10. Matthew 6:33
11. Ephesians 1:13b
12. John 14:3–4
13. John 11:25–26
14. John 10:10

Used with permission by Father Chris Duncan and David D. Libbers. Looked up and quoted from One Touch Bible Soft Computer Program, 2019, www.biblesoft.com.

Table of Contents

Section 1   Fictional Stories That Speak of Life Using Animals or Plants

Section 2   Poems That Are Related to Life and Holidays

Section 3   Poems That Deal with Brokenness, Faith, and God Related to Christianity

Section 4   Poems Related to Brokenness of Life, and Family Related to Christianity

Section 5   Poems Dealing with Faith
in God and Christianity

Section 6   Words That Speak Life in
Voluntary Institutions Other Than Jail

Section 7   Poems Where You See Life

Section 1

Fictional Stories That Speak of Life Using Animals or Plants

The Three Alpacas' Journeys for Their Identities

Once upon a time,
Way down in the great, deep Southern Hemisphere
Lay a farm of humble beginnings.
There on the farm lived three alpacas.
Happy were the alpacas!
Happy were the three!
One was called Snow: she was white and pure
    And known for her long eyelashes.
Another was called Caramel: large in size,
    He was known for causing fights.
The last was the smallest in size:
    His name was Tote;
He was known for being very humble.

For fear of losing their homes, one day
The three alpacas decided to run away!
A journey—they decided to venture out
To find their relative alpaca,
So they could ask who was the greatest of the three
And what their identities were.

They saw their opportunity to begin
This journey they had decided to venture on.
They saw a tractor not far off
To tease. They joked,
"You are too slow!"
The tractor got angry.
"You'll never move

Before the year is up!"
The tractor roared in response,
"I'll show you!"
He began to push slowly forward.
The alpacas danced!
They leaped like deer around the tired old fence.
And suddenly with a loud crash,
The tractor came smashing through
The tired old fence.
Quickly the alpacas dashed off!

The alpacas ran off into the distance.
They ran straight into danger,
For they found themselves in a rain forest
And quickly sinking in quicksand!
Suddenly they cried, "We must turn back!"
But it was too late!
"May God provide us a way out!" prayed Tote,
"A way to escape!"
Suddenly, a bear came through
And offered them a helping hand.
What they did not realize or understand
was the bear wanted them not as friends
But as his next tasty meal plan.
Caramel the alpaca caused trouble, teasing the bear,
And suddenly they all broke loose
While struggling together
To free themselves of the giant bear.

Once scattered about,
The alpacas did run and jump and leap away,
Only to come to their next hurdle,
A bump along the way.
A mountain, this bump was called,

And much to their surprise,
A sign was posted by the base
That frightened them and worried them
At the same time.
BEWARE! it said.
DO NOT CROSS IF YOU DON'T KNOW
    WHO YOU ARE.

Afraid, the alpacas trembled on,
For they must see their way to their alpaca kin
In order to learn who was greatest and where or what their identities
lay in.
They made it to the other side of the mountain safely,
Confused about the sign,
Only to look down and find
A lizard, who was crafty and sly.
"Do not be frightened, for I will take you the rest of the way!"
The lizard said.
"For today is my off day!"

The alpacas soon learned that the danger they feared
    Was not in the mountain itself
But in the small lizard that was their guide.
With deceit, he oiled his way through the desert.
He tried to lead them the wrong way.
He even convinced them that a mirage was real.
That was when Tote cried out,
"Please, Jesus, help us find a way out!"

Straightaway they saw the desert as it was
And ran straight through like a herd of elephants
    And leaping deer too!
And much amazed, they could not believe what lay before them:
The city where their alpaca kin lived within!

"Oh, finally! Finally! At last we are here!"
Cried the three alpacas with glee.
They knocked on the door,
Were invited in,
And met with their relative happily.

Their relative alpaca turned and said to them:

"Do not be fooled; I am no alpaca,
and neither is Caramel, too!
We are larger than the two of you.
That makes us llamas,
A kin animal to both of you, Snow and Tote!
Do not despair;
I have the answer
That you all need to hear.
All of us have a common identity within our own unique personalities.
We are all identified and hidden in Christ;
In Christ is our identity.
In Christ we are secure, accepted, and important too!
For he always provides for us,
Accepts us as we are,
Standing ready to forgive and save us
At any moment in life.
All we have to do
Is receive eternal salvation.
So how do we receive salvation?
We simply ask Jesus Christ to be our personal Lord and Savior
        In our lives,
And then it will be done for us:
We will be saved.
For it is our belief in Christ that we are justified,
And through his strength and by his blood we are saved—

A gift; we simply ask him to write
Our names in the book of life.
If we ask him to write our names
Out of our belief in him and desire to be saved,
Then it is done.
Our faith journey begins:
A lifetime of relationship and love for him.
Accept today!
You will never be happier.
Now you truly know
What is important,
Who you are,
If you accept Christ,
And where your identity should be—
It should be hidden in Christ.
Stand ready to serve Jesus Christ today!
And in the end, you will have lived
The best way that was for you!
Even if it did not turn out the way you expected,
God would never do anything that was not in your best interest,
So trust in him
To love you, to save, to comfort you, to bring you peace.
And choose Christ today!"

That if you confess with your mouth, "Jesus is Lord," and believe in your heart that God raised him from the dead, you will be saved. For it is with your heart that you believe and are justified, and it is with your mouth that you confess and are saved. As the Scripture says, "Anyone who trusts in him will never be put to shame." For there is no difference between Jew and Gentile—the same Lord is Lord of all and richly blesses all who call on him, for,

"Everyone who calls on the name of the Lord will be saved." (**Romans 10:9–13 NIV**)

All that the Father gives Me will come to Me, and the one who comes to Me I will by no means cast out. (**John 6:37 NKJV**)

The Peanut Who Was Impatient

There once lived a tiny peanut who was impatient.
He got upset in everything that he did because whatever he did
    Did not go his way fast enough or at all.
He started off being angry.
"Get into my mouth, you peas!"
He screamed at his dinner.
He stabbed at them angrily,
And they spilled onto the ground.
"No!" he cried. "I want this toy to work!" or "I want it now!"
"Oh, no!" cried Mama Nut.
"That will not do!
It's time-out for you!
Until you can learn to be more patient with your things,
You will always get upset, grumpy, and angry at everything and everyone that gets in your way."

Peanut soon began school.
"That's my eraser! You can't use it! Give it back now!" he cried as he snatched it out of his classmate's hand.
"This will not do!" cried his teacher.
It is off to the principal's office for you!"

"Get on here, glitter and glue," he yelled at his art project.
"Why won't you stick where I want you to?"
The teacher exclaimed,
"It is back to the principal's office for you!"

Then the guidance counselor met with Peanut after school that day.
She thought it would help to explain how Peanut could learn to have an easier time

And make things work the way they should.
She was going to teach him patience.
"You see," she explained as Peanut sat on her couch,
"It is not hard to see.
The answer is plain and ever true.
Just slow down a little when you get upset,
Take a few deep breaths,
And concentrate hard on what you are doing.
And above all, don't get mad!
The moment you get mad, you let impatience win,
And then what you do falls apart
Because you are concentrating on being frustrated
And not what you are doing.
When you are impatient, you are too angry to do anything right.
You can also be very destructive when impatient.
You can destroy the artwork you are trying to create
Or break the things you are trying to fix,
Only for a moment's relief to let your anger out,
To feel better.
But there is a way to feel better and not be impatient,"
Said the guidance counselor.
"When you start to get angry,
Just take a break if you can
And come back when you are calm.
If you can't take a break,
Then tell someone that you are getting frustrated or upset.
Name what you can't do and say what it is.
Just ask for a little help doing it,
Or simply try to take a few deep breaths,
Tell yourself you can do this without getting mad,
And lovingly proceed to do the best you can.
This last way, however, is the least successful
And only works after you have some patience
And have learned some self-control.

Remember, take deep breaths to slow your anger.
Take a break for a while,
Or if it is too much, and you know you need help,
Never be afraid to humble yourself.
Admit that you need help, and just ask!"

"Thanks, that's great advice!"
"You're welcome," replied the guidance counselor.
"But let me leave you with one final warning:
If you do not develop patience, your impatience drives people away,
For in expressing your anger against what you cannot do,
No one wants to be around you.
So get a good handle on your patience,
And all will go reasonably well for you.
You will be ridiculed less along the way;
You'll be a better person, the more patience you gain!"
"Oh, thank you! Thank you!" cried Peanut happily.
"I am going to go forth and try what you talked about today.
Maybe if I am lucky,
I might make a few more friends along the way,
Because I won't drive people off
With getting angry over what I have trouble doing myself,
Or when things don't go my way!"
So Peanut went forth and was a better nut for hearing this advice.

Content Scripture Reference based on Poem's Themes

Patience:

A man's wisdom gives him patience; it is to his glory to overlook an offense. (Proverbs 19:11 NIV)

NIV One Touch Bible Soft Computer Program, 2019, www. biblesoft.com

But the fruit of the Spirit is love, joy, peace, patience, kindness, goodness, faithfulness, gentleness and self-control. Against such things there is no law. Those who belong to Christ Jesus have crucified the sinful nature with its passions and desires. Since we live by the Spirit, let us keep in step with the Spirit. Let us not become conceited, provoking and envying each other. (Galatians 5:22–26 NIV)

NIV One Touch Bible Soft Computer Program, 2019, www. biblesoft.com

Self-Control:

For this very reason, make every effort to add to your faith goodness; and to goodness, knowledge; and to knowledge, self-control; and to self-control, perseverance; and to perseverance, godliness; and to godliness, brotherly kindness; and to brotherly kindness, love. For if you possess these qualities in increasing measure, they will keep you from being ineffective and unproductive in your knowledge of our Lord Jesus Christ. (2 Peter 1:5–9 NIV)

NIV One Touch Bible Soft Computer Program, 2019, www. biblesoft.com

The Lizard Who Was Angry at Rainy Days

There once was a lizard who lived in a small hole.

The hole was hidden under the riverbed at the mouth of a cave.

Every morning, he would come out to look at the sunrise and marvel at the day.

There was just one problem: He did not like rainy days.

Rainy days made him angry.

They made him turn red, and his eyes were all yellow.

His breath was like fire when he yelled at a rainy morning, "Rainy morning go away! Never come again another day!"

Sunny days were pretty and tropical where he lived.

Although he lived on the water's edge, he did not like to feel water rain down on him hard.

Oh, what would the lizard do with his anger, with his problem?

He would have to face what made him angry, what he did not always like some days, while other days the problem was not there.

The answer was plain: He had to learn to calm down and control his temper. He had to learn to accept rainy days even though he did not like them.

How would he do this?

"I know!" cried the lizard. "I will go ask my neighbor the beaver."

The lizard shouted at the next rainy day,

"I'll know how to conquer you yet, rainy day! Then I won't be angry anymore!" He roared as he turned red.

So the lizard went to see his neighbor the beaver.

The beaver was out swimming around in the rain, happily working on his house.

"Mr. Beaver," said the lizard, "How do you deal with those horrible rainy days?"

"Why, rainy days aren't horrible to me," replied Mr. Beaver. "I love them as much as you love sunny days. I like to play in the water and in the rain!"

"What!" roared the lizard.

"How can anyone like rainy days?"

"That is simple," replied the beaver. "It is all on perspective. Perspective is how you view something.

Simply change your view on how you see the world as a rainy day, and you won't get mad at rainy days anymore."

"Oh, thank you, Mr. Beaver. I'd knew you'd have the answer.

But how do you change—what is the word?—perspective?"

"That is simple. Learn to make it a habit of purposefully thinking of a different emotion than anger every time you see a rainy morning greet you, and pretty soon, you will automatically think of that emotion every rainy morning that follows. Just choose your emotion wisely and make it a habit, and your anger will go away in no time!"

"Thank you, Mr. Beaver," replied the lizard.

The lizard went home and learned to think blue thoughts by turning blue every morning that it rained for several months.

Then he went back to Mr. Beaver in despair and said, "Mr. Beaver, I have been thinking blue thoughts and turning blue when it rains. Now I feel blue and down whenever I see a rainy day instead of anger."

"I told you," replied the beaver, "to choose your emotion carefully. Why don't you think yellow thoughts instead?"

"What do you mean yellow thoughts?"

"Learn to tell yourself you will make the most of this rainy day, and look for the sunshine amid the rainy day."

"That's preposterous!" replied the lizard. "How can it be a sunny day and a rainy day at the same time?"

"No, no, you've got it wrong, lizard!

I said look for the sunny day within the rainy one.

That means look for all of the good that occurs in that day even though it is raining, and learn to be grateful for life. If you do that, soon your rainy day will look a whole lot sunnier, and then you will never truly have to deal with a rainy day again! You will have conquered your anger and your problem by finding the sunny day within the rainy day!"

"How wonderful!" replied the lizard.

So the lizard went forth happy and always looked for any good that could be found when things were bad, or for something positive that was there when things seemed negative. He went forth with a better outlook on life and was a happy lizard who never again struggled with being angry at a rainy day.

Content Scripture Reference Based on Poem's Themes

Anger:

The Lord is compassionate and gracious, slow to anger, abounding in love. He will not always accuse, nor will he harbor his anger forever. (Psalms 103:8–9 NIV)

NIV One Touch Bible Soft Computer Program, 2019, www. biblesoft.com

"In your anger do not sin": Do not let the sun go down while you are still angry, and do not give the devil a foothold. He who has been stealing must steal no longer, but must work, doing something useful with his own hands, that he may have something to share with those in need. (Ephesians 4:26–28 NIV)

NIV One Touch Bible Soft Computer Program, 2019, www. biblesoft.com

The Bird Named Cheetos Who Did Not Share

Once upon a time in the remote town of Laplace, Louisiana, was a gas station.

At the gas station, many things went on that onlookers did not always notice.

One such activity was the interaction of the local adopted gas station cat, who lived in

The bushes by the gas station.

The cat's name was Pickles.

Pickles was scrawny and always trying to steal food from the local birds, who ate stray food that landed

On the ground at the gas station.

One day, several birds were fighting over a bunch of Cheetos that were scattered about the ground.

One bird, who was small in size, proudly scarfed his Cheetos, which turned his beak from red to orange.

Pickles was nearby, swishing his tail, and approached the scrawny bird.

"I think I'll call you Cheetos, scrawny bird."

"Why?" asked the scrawny bird.

"You were so greedy with those Cheetos that you left none to share with me. Look! See, you ate so many it

Turned your beak orange! You are filled while I am starving!"

"That' not very nice," replied scrawny bird. "But I guess it fits me so I'll accept the name." For scrawny

Had one big fault: He believed whatever people told him. He was easily led to do whatever others wanted even if it was not true or good for him.

"Next time, will you not be so greedy and share some with a scrawny, starving cat?' "We have to eat too,
     you know."
"Okay, well, I don't see why not." The scrawny bird also had another fault: He lacked the ability to see
     Any potential harm coming his way because he was so easily fooled.
"Perhaps I misjudged you. You are not greedy if you share, and are truly willing to share.
     I am sorry," Pickles hissed.
The next day, Cheetos where thrown on the ground.
Pickles ran into a crowd of fighting birds.
They all flew off except Cheetos.
The other birds were cautious and knew not to risk trusting a cat.
For a cat was a stranger, and in their
     case a predator. Where there is a stranger, danger can be found.
     Cheetos, wanting to please Pickles and gain a friend, had pity on the cat, and not wanting to be greedy and wanting to share, he took a risk and stayed.
Cheetos asked Pickles, "Why did you scare off the other birds if we were all supposed to share?"
"Oh, only to have more to share between you, and ... meal ..."
"What?" asked Cheetos.
"I am sorry, I meant between you and me. I guess I am so hungry thinking about food that I accidentally
     said the wrong word."
"Oh, okay," said Cheetos blindly, gullibly not sensing any danger and not being afraid when he should have
     felt nervous.
Cheetos said, "Well, let me break the remaining Cheetos with my beak, and half of them will be for you,
and half of them will be for me."
By the time Cheetos had made it to breaking the last Cheeto in half, he was suddenly no more, for he

was swallowed up whole by Pickles, who then ate all of the Cheetos for himself. He sat down, licked his paws, and got up and walked away slowly like he had not done anything.

The other birds looked for Cheetos when Pickles had left but could find him no more, for he had

> Trusted a cat, a stranger, and a wrong character—he trusted an animal known to prey on birds.

The other birds went along with their lives at the gas station. They lived long lives because they knew not to trust strangers!

Note to the Reader: Extremely Important—Please Read!

Pickles was an evil cat and so clever that he was not only dangerous, in that he planned to eat Cheetos from the beginning, but that he convinced Cheetos that he had the character of greed and selfishness, which were really the character that Pickles had. Pickles did not care what happened to Cheetos, who was a stranger, and all Pickles cared about was what he wanted, which was his next meal plan. This is why strangers are so dangerous: You do not know them, who they are, or what they are like. This automatically makes them dangerous because you cannot tell whether they will cause you harm because you do not know anything about them.

The next time you see a stranger approach children and talk to them, be sure to call the police. Write down their license plate if they are in a car and if you are able. Above all, don't keep it a secret, even if they tell you to—especially if they tell you to! They may be planning to snatch you away from your parents, especially if they want to keep seeing you and you have not told anyone. If you are a child, and you see another child talking to a stranger, if you are not too young, help and be a hero! Go tell a teacher, a parent, a close friend, or a neighbor—someone you know well who is trusted by your family. Give a description of who was talking to whom, and tell them you don't know this adult who is talking to your friend. The teacher, neighbor, parent, or trusted friend will know where to take it from there. "Stranger Danger," as the old slogan goes. It's still as true today as it was yesterday. Remember to reach out a hand and help your friend in need!

Content Scripture Reference Based on Poem's Themes

Pride:

"The pride of your heart has deceived you, you who live in the clefts of the rocks and make your home on the heights, you who say to yourself, 'Who can bring me down to the ground?' Though you soar like the eagle and make your nest among the stars, from there I will bring you down," declares the Lord. (Obadiah 1:3–4 NIV)

NIV One Touch Bible Soft Computer Program, 2019, www.biblesoft.com

Greed:

Watch out! Be on your guard against all kinds of greed; a man's life does not consist in the abundance of his possessions. (Luke 12:15 NIV)

NIV One Touch Bible Soft Computer Program, 2019, www.biblesoft.com

The Emotional Daisy That Needed to Learn to Grow

Faraway overseas existed a special place in the highlands.

It was the most beautiful field you have ever seen, especially in the spring time.

It was lush and green and full of dandelions, and unusually enough, a single Daisy grew here.

The Daisy felt shame because she was different from the dandelions. She could not see the unique beauty that existed within her that made her a Daisy.

She was clothed with golden petals and a brown center.

She would often look around as the weather shifted from winter to spring, watching the dandelions blow away.

She envied them because although they were white and could float in a cluster, they stuck together as they were carried away by the wind.

Daisy did not realize that when the dandelions were carried away by the wind, it was a form of death for them. They would land on the ground somewhere, and if they were lucky, God would water them into the ground, and they would die.

When they died, they created more dandelions.

The dandelions in this particular meadow were special.

They were made up of different kinds of seeds within themselves— all kinds.

Though dandelions are often thought of as weeds, the seeds of the dandelions were what were most important about them. What type of seed were they going to sow?

Where they going to sow seeds for the kingdom of heaven, or were they going to ignore it and live for themselves?

Some of these dandelion seeds would sow for the kingdom of heaven, but would die not having done anything for God.

When they blew away and died, if they did not sow for the kingdom of heaven, they grew up to be a dandelion flower. They grew up be a weed, which is a form of a tare.

Tares and wheat grow up together. Tares do not live for the kingdom of heaven, so when they die, they are thrown into a fiery furnace and burned up like chaff.

In this sense, for the dandelions that sowed their seeds for the kingdom of heaven, they became a sort of wheat in that they yielded good seed because they sowed the seed of the word of God to the world.

Daisy did not realize that she did not have to blow away to sow good seed like the dandelions did. She could sow good seed right where she was.

She did not realize what type of seed she originally came from.

Her seed was planted in good soil, deliberately and with care, so that she would spring up a daisy.

There are many types of seeds that can be sown, but the best seeds are the ones that fall in good soil, where the word of God takes root.

If the word of God, which is a seed, falls on good soil, this seed will die and germinate. Then it will be spread to the ends of the earth.

The individual, who is the good soil the seed (which is the word of God) landed on, will grow because God grows this seed that has died and germinated to grow into a flower.

When the word of God, or seed, is cultivated to grow in an individual's life, that individual will have the word of God written, or planted, in their hearts.

Once cultivated enough, if the word has been "feeding the soil" regularly through studying the word of God, then that individual who has the seed, or word of God, sown in their hearts goes forth and sows more seeds.

The purpose of sowing more seeds is so that more people come to love, trust, and admire God and receive salvation.

Such was the love of Daisy.

Daisy was lovingly planted by the farmer, who grew her in the middle of the field—a remarkable sight and a turned gift to see, when the flower matures and the word of God is spread.

Daisy did not know the farmer.

Daisy felt shame and sorrow most days because she not could not understand why she could not blow away with the dandelions and be like them at the last chill of the winter.

She was always sad when she watched.

She did not realize it was their time to go forth and sow their seeds about the earth.

"I want to be like them.

I am not beautiful."

But Daisy was beautiful in her own way.

What Daisy was missing was experiencing the joy of the gift of life, or eternal salvation, and feeling a deep connection to God.

How would Daisy find this connection?

Daisy began talking to the dandelions one day as they grew back each year, and she learned of their going forth and spreading their seeds throughout God's creation.

Daisy longed to fulfill this purpose so that she too could blow away and share God's word throughout creation.

Daisy did not realize that she did not need to be the same as the dandelions to do the same thing they did. She could tell all of creation around her of God's gift of salvation—that if you ask Jesus Christ to be your personal Lord and Savior out of your desire from within to go to heaven, because you believe Jesus died for all you did wrong, you will be saved.

One day, a dandelion suggested to her that she tell all of creation from where she was planted. She did all she could do for God.

She began to feel a common bond with a flower so different.

Daisy was unsure whether she should take the dandelion's advice.

If she chose to serve God for her purpose—to tell people about him— she would feel that she had a common bond with the dandelion.

She began to feel like she was okay with not blowing away and being exactly like the dandelion—her being her own unique flower with a similar purpose done a different way was okay.

The only problem was that Daisy was unsure whether she should follow this advice because she lacked a connection with God.

Then one day, Daisy experienced a new connection.

The farmer who planted her came by, admired her, and lovingly watered her.

It was then that she realized that God was very much like that farmer.

He grew her in the meadow, and he loved her.

It was this experience that helped Daisy realize just how special each individual is and how much God loves each and every individual for who they are. He wants them to come to heaven to live in comfort, peace, and love with him, when they have served their purpose on earth.

Then Daisy knew the most important thing she could do as a daisy, and she was very excited!

She was going to follow the dandelion's suggestion and tell all of creation around her about God.

She could tell everyone of this love that God had for her, and for them too.

She was so excited that she started telling the dandelions who had been making it a practice to spread good seed, and when they blew away and died, as they were floating off, they proclaimed the good news of the kingdom of heaven to all of the creation around them.

Now all of creation, as their seeds are spread, could be spreading the word of God!

Because all Daisy did every day was sit there, she got to work with her new task.

She felt love, which God cultivated in her life.

She felt the joy of salvation in her heart because she was eagerly and excitingly telling the dandelions about God, as well as all of creation that surrounded her or came to visit her.

Daisy no longer felt shame and sorrow about not being able to blow away like the dandelions, and her beauty grew through her love for God and how she spread it, making the outside look even more beautiful than before.

Now every winter, when the dandelions blow away in the meadow at the last chill, she excitedly wishes them the best and makes sure that they tell people about God.

They always shout back at her as they float off that they will tell people about God!

Daisy knew that not all of the dandelions would tell people about God. Not all of the dandelion would fall on good soil. Some would die, fall, on bad soil, and are no more.

Although sad, this is part of life.

Seeds that fall on bad soil grow up to be tares. Tares are thrown into the fire and burned up by God. Tares are not thrown into the fire until after they die because if they were thrown in the fire while they were among the wheat or good seeds, then the good seed would get burned up with them.

Daisy went on loving life and doing all she could to further God's kingdom and spread the word of God.

A Note to the Reader

See the parable of the sower in any one of the gospels in the New Testament: Matthew, Mark, Luke, or John. Read, study, and analyze the parable of the sower and the seed in its entirety for help with this poem.

Content Scripture References Based on the Poem's Themes

Wheat, tare, and the parable of the sower according to Matthew:

He told them another parable: "The kingdom of heaven is like a mustard seed, which a man took and planted in his field. Though it is the smallest of all your seeds, yet when it grows, it is the largest of garden plants and becomes a tree, so that the birds of the air come and perch in its branches." (Matthew 13:31–32 NIV)

NIV One Touch Bible Soft Computer Program, 2019, www. biblesoft.com

John 12:24-26

I tell you the truth, unless a kernel of wheat falls to the ground and dies, it remains only a single seed. But if it dies, it produces many seeds. The man who loves his life will lose it, while the man who hates his life in this world will keep it for eternal life. Whoever serves me must follow me; and where I am, my servant also will be. My Father will honor the one who serves me. (John 12:24–26 NIV)

NIV One Touch Bible Soft Computer Program, 2019, www. biblesoft.com

Receiving Salvation:

But what does it say? "The word is near you; it is in your mouth and in your heart," that is, the word of faith we are proclaiming: That if you confess with your mouth, "Jesus is Lord," and believe in your heart that God raised him from the dead, you will be saved. For it is with your heart that you believe and are justified, and it is with your mouth that you confess and are saved. As the Scripture says, "Anyone who trusts in him will never be put to shame." For there is no difference between Jew and Gentile — the same Lord is Lord of all and richly blesses all who call on him, for, "Everyone who calls on the name of the Lord will be saved." (Romans 10:8–13 NIV)

NIV One Touch Bible Soft Computer Program, 2019, www. biblesoft.com

John 6:37

All that the Father gives Me will come to Me, and the one who comes to Me I will by no means cast out. (John 6:37 NKJV)

NKJV One Touch Bible Soft Computer Program, 2019, www. biblesoft.com

Scripture Reference

The poem is partially built around this parable scripture; partial quotes and ideas were used.

The Parable of the Sower:

"Listen then to what the parable of the sower means: When anyone hears the message about the kingdom and does not understand it, the evil one comes and snatches away what was sown in his heart. This is the seed sown along the path. The one who received the seed that fell on rocky places is the man who hears the word and at once receives it with joy. But since he has no root, he lasts only a short time. When trouble or persecution comes because of the word, he quickly falls away. The one who received the seed that fell among the thorns is the man who hears the word, but the worries of this life and the deceitfulness of wealth choke it, making it unfruitful. But the one who received the seed that fell on good soil is the man who hears the word and understands it. He produces a crop, yielding a hundred, sixty or thirty times what was sown."

Jesus told them another parable: "The kingdom of heaven is like a man who sowed good seed in his field. But while everyone was sleeping, his enemy came and sowed weeds among the wheat, and went away. When the wheat sprouted and formed heads, then the weeds also appeared.

"The owner's servants came to him and said, 'Sir, didn't you sow good seed in your field? Where then did the weeds come from?'

"'An enemy did this,' he replied.

"The servants asked him, 'Do you want us to go and pull them up?'

"'No,' he answered, 'because while you are pulling the weeds, you may root up the wheat with them. Let both grow together until the harvest. At that time, I will tell the harvesters: First collect the weeds and tie them in bundles to be burned; then gather the wheat and bring it into my barn.'" (Matthew 13:18–30 NIV)

NIV One Touch Bible Soft Computer Program, 2019, www. biblesoft.com

The Onion Who Learned to Cry

There once was an onion named Skunk.

Skunk lived in an onion patch on a farm.

Skunk's mother would always talk to him when the sun rose.

She spoke of things that did not seem real.

They were worlds away from Skunk, but they all seemed like nightmares.

She spoke of salads, kitchens, and shopping bags, and worst of all, the end: getting eaten.

She told Skunk that getting eaten by someone was part of life; if you weren't eaten, you got thrown

Away where no one would love you.

Then you would feel alone, abandoned, and forsaken as you rotted to death with the garbage.

These stories frightened Skunk.

Though he was frightened, he simply could not cry.

He could not cry when he thought of how his life would end.

He saw it as his life ending in order to make someone else happy and to become part of the food chain.

There was just one problem: Skunk's mother did not realize that Skunk would have a very different ending.

One day, Skunk got picked from the onion patch.

He was loaded onto a truck, where he was taken to a fruit stand, washed off, and placed out in a bin of other white onions for sale.

A day later, he was sold.

He was placed in a shopping bag and taken to the owner's home.

The owner began preparing dinner that night.

Skunk wondered whether dinner that night would mean his end.

What would he do if it was the end?

He suddenly became fearful.

He still was unable to cry.

Because he could not cry, he could not overcome the problems within himself.

The frightened onion was approached by the owner with a knife.

He began to tremble.

He was so frightened that he actually made himself roll.

He rolled unto a spoon meant for a stew, with the owner in hot pursuit of the onion.

The owner banged his hand down to try to stop the onion so he could pick him up, but missed.

Instead, he hit the other end of the spoon.

Suddenly, Skunk was airborne.

He thought that he was having one last thrill before he met his end.

All of a sudden, the owner looked behind him as he heard a splat.

The onion had landed in the owner's cake!

"Oh, no!" cried the owner. "My cake! It is ruined!

No one is going to eat onion cake!

Now I have to go back to the store for supplies, but I'll buy take-out for tonight."

"Out to the garbage you go, like the garbage you are!" the owner yelled at the onion and the cake.

The onion began to cry as he was heaved into the darkness.

Then he felt better, and all of the sudden, he felt love!

This cake had saved his life!

The two were an unlikely pair, but in welcoming each other as friends, they managed to save each other from being eaten by ruining the way the tasted to their owners.

As the onion settled in the garbage dump for the city, a week later, Skunk was still with the cake.

The cake and Skunk loved each other as friends, and they rotted together until they were no more, loving each other because they saved each other from a worse fate: getting eaten. In doing so, they loved each other as themselves, as neighbors.

In the end, Skunk died in a trash heap, but he was not alone. He overcame his problems, he learned to cry, and he learned to love others as himself by learning to love the most unlikely item of food like himself that was simply a misfit with an onion: a white cake with almond buttercream frosting.

Content Scripture Reference Based on Poem's Themes

Love Your Neighbor as Yourself:

Jesus replied: "'Love the Lord your God with all your heart and with all your soul and with all your mind.' This is the first and greatest commandment. And the second is like it: 'Love your neighbor as yourself.' All the Law and the Prophets hang on these two commandments." (Matthew 22:37–40 NIV)

NIV One Touch Bible Soft Computer Program, 2019, www. biblesoft.com

Fear:

The fear of the Lord is pure, enduring forever. The ordinances of the Lord are sure and altogether righteous. (Psalm 19:9 NIV)

NIV One Touch Bible Soft Computer Program, 2019, www. biblesoft.com

Section 2

Poems That Are Related to Life and Holidays

The Department Store Santa with Bad Teeth

There once was a department store Santa who had bad teeth.
He was sloppy and did not care about his teeth.
He went to work one day—
A mistake he would not count on making.
He grabbed his belly while on the floor to practice his jolly laugh,
Which proved to be a fatal mistake.
"Ho, Ho, Ho!" he cried
While looking all around.
Much to his surprise, he then realized
A small crowd had gathered around.
"Just look at his teeth!" one commented.
"Does he ever brush?"
"They look like the Grinch who stole Christmas!" said another in a
loud murmur.

Much to his embarrassment,
The department store Santa looked downtrodden.
Suddenly, a manager appeared from around the corner.
"What is all of this,
Department Store Santa?
These people are not lining up to sit in your lap!
They are lining up to mock your bad teeth!
You're fired! And don't come back until you have some dental work
that is a success."

Tearful and blue, the department store Santa and went home,
But along the way,
He bought a cheap toothbrush and some cheap toothpaste.

He stood in front of the mirror and stared.

"Oh, how will I brush? Or make up for years and years of lack of dental work."

Then much to his surprise, a Christmas miracle did occur.

The toothbrush! It spoke! It came to life!

"I am here to help you!" exclaimed the green toothbrush.

"To help your teeth become a few shades lighter!

I am here to brush your teeth!"

Frightened, Santa stumbled back,

And the toothpaste landed upon his cheap toothbrush.

The toothbrush lunged forward and began to brush his teeth.

Once finished, his once green teeth looked a little yellow, but much improved.

Santa wondered, "How did this Christmas wish, this Christmas miracle, come through?"

Ahead he looked and was much amazed.

The toothpaste had left written instructions on how to brush his teeth!

He followed the directions every day

Religiously for a year.

And by the holiday season the next year,

His teeth were in much better shape!

He went back to the department store that fired him

And burst into the manager's office.

"I am back now and better than before. See? Just look at my teeth!

They are a light yellow after a year of brushing!

I think this will not scare the public, or little kids!"

"Okay," agreed the manager, "it will do."

He hired him back as an on-call seasonal worker—and on-call Santa too.

He went to the floor and sat in Santa's chair.

The crowd lined up.

They were all smiles too.

The children sat upon his lap and told him what they wanted.

He played the role to help the real Santa out so perfectly.
And when his first day was up, he wondered why no one remembered him
As the department store Santa with bad teeth.
Then he realized that it is not always best to be noticed by others if it is in a bad or embarrassing way.
It is important to always do what you should
And blend in when it comes to oral hygiene.
Being noticed will make you only feel bad,
Will make you feel blue.
So at the very best,
If you don't know how to brush your teeth,
Just look for videos on the Internet.
And buy a tooth brush, preferably an electric one because it cleans better.
And brush your teeth with whitening toothpaste every day.
You'll be better for it
And never have to suffer the embarrassment
That department store Santa did one year!

Content Scripture Reference Based on Poem's Themes

Love Your Neighbor as Yourself:
Jesus replied: "'Love the Lord your God with all your heart and with all your soul and with all your mind.' This is the first and greatest commandment. 39 And the second is like it: 'Love your neighbor as yourself.' All the Law and the Prophets hang on these two commandments." (Matthew 22:37–40 NIV)
NIV One Touch Bible Soft Computer Program, 2019, www. biblesoft.com

Tank the Christmas Cat's Sleigh Ride

There once was a scrawny neighborhood black cat.
Little did he know that he would get a new name and a new home one day.
His original owners did not feed him enough to suit him because he had a big appetite.
Because of the cat feeling neglected not only by way of food but by way of love,
    He ran away one day.
He lived on the neighborhood streets, fighting other neighborhood cats and stealing any food left out.
He was on a mission to find love, food, and a new home too—he was in search of a committee.
Finally, one day he found his committee—a dream come true!
A home that gave him love and all the food he could imagine too!
One fall, the Christmas parade approached, and the cat now called Tank, for he ate four bowls a day,
    Desired to be in the Christmas parade.
He thought,
"If included,
I'll be loved, and respected even more!
I must be a part of the Christmas joy!"
So, when Santa's sleigh—the fire brigade—came roaring down the street, collecting canned goods and giving out treats,
Tank ran up to the fire sleigh and hopped on!
Much to Santa's surprise,
A black cat
Did climb up his white beard
And spread his paws around his neck to give him a big hug!

The fire brigade kept on going, and soon Santa could not see
Because Tank was loving him so much, his eyes were covered!
Around the neighborhood the fire sleigh zoomed!
Santa had begun to fret.
"Whatever shall I do?" asked Santa.
"I know!" said Santa with much delight.
He had the fire sleigh double back to the place where the cat jumped on.
His family was waiting for him there,
And they were much relieved.
Santa stopped the fire sleigh
And asked,
"What do you want for Christmas, Tank?"
Tank looked over, and much to his surprise,
There was a bit of catnip hanging off the side of the fire sleigh.
Tank rushed over and started to play!
"Okay!" chuckled Santa with a twinkle in his eye.
"You've been a good boy, Tank! You've had a hard life and found a new home!
Catnip it is!" He reached over and gave the catnip to Tank.
Tank jumped down and looked back up, purring at Santa Claus.
Tank loved so much, and he finally felt love.
He got all the food and attention a cat could ask for.
"I think," said Santa as the fire sleigh began to start up again,
"That Tank is a very special indeed!
A cat that shows love by giving hugs
Seems very thankful indeed!
Take care of him. He is very special for all the love he has to give.
Most cats that are starved and later find homes
Don't necessarily have all that love to give!"
The family was so happy that Tank was rewarded with the gift of his choice
That they donated all the canned goods in their pantry for Santa's cause.

And then with a crack of his whip and a "Ho! Ho! Ho!" Santa took off to the next neighborhood.

What most people often forget is that when you show love to others, you feel loved

   Because you love others, expecting nothing in return.

It is the way to show someone you care; you feel love and warmth in your heart even if they don't return it!

So take heed and learn from this special Christmas cat. Tank loved and found all the love he could ever want by loving others first and expecting nothing back!

Content Scripture Reference Based on Poem's Themes

Love Your Neighbor as Yourself:

Jesus replied: "'Love the Lord your God with all your heart and with all your soul and with all your mind.' This is the first and greatest commandment. And the second is like it: 'Love your neighbor as yourself.' All the Law and the Prophets hang on these two commandments." (Matthew 22:37–40 NIV)

NIV One Touch Bible Soft Computer Program, 2019, www. biblesoft.com

The Easter Bunny That Ate Too Many Peeps

There once was an Easter bunny who loved to eat Peeps.
His favorite Peeps were yellow, which looked like yellow chickadees.
Early one spring, the rabbit did not know
That he would learn his lesson about eating too many Peeps.
The Easter bunny came upon the churchyard on Easter Sunday.
There were children all around; he was going to have an Easter egg hunt.
The rabbit hid and watched the adults, much to his delight,
Stuff plastic Easter eggs with yellow, sugary chickadee Peeps.
"My favorite!" squealed the rabbit in a hushed manner with much delight.
"I've just got to have those peeps!
I'm so hungry!"
Thought the Easter bunny.
"I know!" he thought. "I'll enter the Easter egg hunt in such a way
That no one will notice me!"
The hunt was on!
The children raced forward without delay.
The rabbit kept tucked away, hidden out of sight,
By always hopping behind the trees.
For Easter bunnies are supposed to be hidden from sight,
Never to be seen.
Much to the rabbit's embarrassment,
Little did he know
He would soon be seen!
"What's that?" cried a child.
Another one stuttered.
The children looked onward and could not believe their eyes,

For what a sight that did behold them!
A fat Easter bunny hiding behind a tree!
He had gathered all the eggs in the hunt,
Which led all the children straight to him!
One by one, he gulped the little Peep chickadees out of each Easter egg!
"What a greedy rabbit!" cried the little children.
"He's left none to share!
Oh, however did this happen?
However, did he get here?"
"I don't know," cried another child.
"What is going on here?" said an ominous voice.
It was an adult, and the children had turned around to stare at her.
But when they looked back,
The rabbit was gone!
"We know we just saw a greedy Easter rabbit eat all of our chickadee Peeps from our eggs!"
"Preposterous!" cried the adult.
The children looked back and saw a pile of empty eggs.
A trail of Peeps led all the way to a rabbit hole!
The adult followed suit and finally gave up with a sigh.
"Okay, I believe you all, children!
But what did you learn here?
Stealing no matter how small is wrong.
Greed gets you nowhere. You get fat like that rabbit, if it's gluttony that's your problem!
If you steal, you will get caught,
And if you overeat, your body will show it!
It's best to do what you can to improve yourself,
Even if it's not perfect!
No person's body is shaped perfectly.
We are all unique!
Just because your body is not perfect, even if it is bigger, that does not make you bad or gluttonous!

Many people have many problems in many different forms!
And people who steal not only take things away from others,
They rob them of the joy that object brought them, the peace of mind that they had when it was in their possession. They cause themselves anxiety and worry because they no longer have it!
So think hard and take heed not to be greedy or steal like this imposter Easter bunny!
For the real Easter bunny would not be so unkind to children.
Remember your lessons you learned here,
And you will save yourself some heartache, grief, and despair,
Which may never happen because you chose to not learn the hard way
And to listen other's advice!"
"Hooray!" cried the children.
"We've learned a lot.
We actually feel sorry for the Easter rabbit,
Who struggled not to eat too many chickadee Peeps!
Thank you for sharing your knowledge with us
And saving us from trouble a little later!"

Content Scripture Reference Based on Poem's Themes

Greed:

Watch out! Be on your guard against all kinds of greed; a man's life does not consist in the abundance of his possessions. (Luke 12:15 NIV)

NIV One Touch Bible Soft Computer Program, 2019, www. biblesoft.com

Not Sharing:

If I have kept my bread to myself, not sharing it with the fatherless—but from my youth I reared him as would a father, and from my birth I guided the widow—if I have seen anyone perishing for lack of clothing, or a needy man without a garment, and his heart did not bless me for warming him with the fleece from my sheep, if I have raised my hand against the fatherless, knowing that I had influence in court, then let my arm fall from the shoulder, let it be broken off at the joint. (Job 31:17–22 NIV)

NIV One Touch Bible Soft Computer Program, 2019, www.biblesoft.com

Stealing:

He who has been stealing must steal no longer, but must work, doing something useful with his own hands, that he may have something to share with those in need. (Ephesians 4:28 NIV)

NIV One Touch Bible Soft Computer Program, 2019, www.biblesoft.com

Gluttony:

When you sit to dine with a ruler, note well what is before you, and put a knife to your throat if you are given to gluttony. Do not crave his delicacies, for that food is deceptive.

Do not wear yourself out to get rich; have the wisdom to show restraint. Cast but a glance at riches, and they are gone, for they will surely sprout wings and fly off to the sky like an eagle.

Do not eat the food of a stingy man, do not crave his delicacies; for he is the kind of man who is always thinking about the cost. "Eat and drink," he says to you, but his heart is not with you. You will vomit up the little you have eaten and will have wasted your compliments.

Do not speak to a fool, for he will scorn the wisdom of your words. (Proverbs 23:1–9 NIV)

NIV One Touch Bible Soft Computer Program, 2019, www. biblesoft.com

Orange Cream and an Irish Dream—A St. Patrick's Day Poem

Orange cream in swirly clouds,
Gumdrop oranges,
They all surround!

Rivers of orange sugar flow through the ground!
Surrounded by laughing taffy trees!
The taffy trees,
They never surmise,
Or wonder, or ponder,
Or see their own demise!

I ride swiftly on the back of a cotton candy airplane made of bright
orange candy.
I ride upon the swirly clouds.
Then suddenly my orange cotton candy airplane disappears
beneath me!
I fall suddenly!
I plummet
Into the river of orange sugar!
It flows quickly through the land of orange laughing taffy trees.
It carries me out into the orange sea!
Will I drown?
You, English horizon—your orange shore!
You remain behind me!
Will peace draw near?
Yes, there will be peace again one day, like never before!

Oh, Ireland, your candies of mints come and wash up with me upon
the orange beach's shore.
To our orange candy beaches of the English,
Together, to this day we remain and mingle,
A part of each other's lives, the English of orange and the Irish of
green,
Living a modern-day dream of peace and harmony.
Although not quite perfect peace every day,
We strive to obtain it every day
Anyway!
Our candies mix together, bring a new taste!
A new freedom!
A new reign!

At the end of every day,
Let the Irish and the English
Come together united as neighbors in brotherhood and sisterhood
And pray as one people,
Together one day,
In a dream of peace,
To share always
And forevermore,
We will pray:
May every dawn of every day
Never bring pain again to us the next day.
May pain and bloodshed never return or creep in
By the last moment of every sunset of every day!
Let it remain between us
This way
Forevermore and always!

Content Reference Based on Poem's Themes

Peace:

Peace I leave with you; my peace I give you. I do not give to you as the world gives. Do not let your hearts be troubled and do not be afraid. "You heard me say, 'I am going away and I am coming back to you.' If you loved me, you would be glad that I am going to the Father, for the Father is greater than I. I have told you now before it happens, so that when it does happen you will believe. (John 14:27–30 NIV)

NIV One Touch Bible Soft Computer Program, 2019, www. biblesoft.com

Section 3

Poems That Deal with Brokenness, Faith, and God Related to Christianity

Oh, Return! My Soul! To Be a Well-Watered Garden of Life!

I look up at the sky
Only to shield my eyes
At the wonder of a beautiful day.

Green grass all around;
Spring is on the ground!
And soon good things are to come—
Only when you look for them!

The surf of the ocean under your feet,
A gentle breeze,
Caressing your cheek.

As you feel the summer's scorching heat,
You do not focus on the sweltering heat the day brings.
No! Negativity!
You focus on the gentle breeze that cools you down,
If only for one moment,
Throughout the summer's scorching day!

These are all good things that are easy and plan to see,
As long as one pays attention to what encompasses the physical
surroundings of one's day!

Perhaps it is right!
Yes, good to focus on right things!
And if you do,
Pretty soon

The bad things will be chased away!

This does not mean that the bad is completely gone.
It means that you do not focus on what is bad.
For what is bad darkens the soul,
Blackens the mood,
Causes utter hatred and bitterness to grow within the soul.

Injustices occur every day all of the time.
Things that aren't fair in life always happen, every day.
The more you focus on what was unfair or what injustices were done
to you,
The angrier you will be all of the time
Eventually,
And one day you will wake up
And ask yourself,
"Why and how did I ever come to have such hate within my heart?
Such bitterness, such blackness within?
For all that spews from my mouth nowadays
Is the venom of hatred, bitterness, anger, and negativity.

So how do I return to the beauty of life and begin to learn to see the
good in life, and no longer hate?"
The answer is simple:
Return to the early morning days in your life.

Return to a simpler time in life,
Where you were capable of noticing the beauty of God's creation
And loving all other initially in this world for who they were, no
matter what they have done.

"But how?" you say,
"Do I return to this day?

If I cannot see past my anger at an individual who has caused me a great injustice,
Whom I struggle to forgive?"

The answer is simple:
Ask Jesus Christ to consider that person forgiven in your book on your behalf.
Ask Jesus Christ to give you the ability to forgive that person in your heart, believe that you will receive this, and you will.
Next, drop all opinions of the individual or persons.
Tell yourself that you refuse to think about former opinions of them or form new ones.
Then simply move forward in a relationship with that person by Focusing only on present things you do with them or pleasant topics you know you will not argue on.
Stay away from topics you argue on with this person, form no opinions no matter what already transpired, and stick to pleasant and present-minded topics of conversations and activities.

Do this, and after a while, you will be able to move on in the face of injustice.
You will eventually be able to forgive this person in your heart, but only if you believe that Jesus gave you that ability will you have your moment of epiphany!

"Try all of these things, and things will fare well?
So what do you mean, return to the early morning days of your life?"
Return to when love was new, when you found the good in life every day, no matter what happened.
Return when you were happy to experience life with vivacious curiosity and unending growth.
And pretty soon,
You soul will be a well-watered garden again,
But only by God's grace and power.

Scripture Reference Based on Quoted Scripture the Poem Is Based On

You will be like a well-watered garden, like a spring whose waters never fail. (Isaiah 58:11b NIV)

NIV One Touch Bible Soft Computer Program, 2019, www.biblesoft.com

God Loves You in Your Yesterdays, Todays, and Tomorrows

Yesterday was my brighter future.
Yesterday, I had a greater hope for tomorrow.
Yesterday, love was new.
Yesterday, life was new.

Yesterday, my family loved me.
Yesterday, my family and I grew in loving one another together.
Strongly united in yesterday's bonds
Was my family and I,
Only for them to be destroyed by the future's many disappointments.
Now, yesterday's strong family bonds are all gone.

Deep within the darkness,
In the shadow of my mind,
I see the broken shards of past memories.
I see many yesterdays long past.
In these yesterdays that did not last,
I see warm sunshine, clear blue skies,
The laughter of delight and sharing, untied in love and happiness
by my family,
Long since forgotten.
Long since passed.
I see brothers and sisters, mothers and daughters, fathers and sons,
All walking together in the early morning shores in the warm
sunshine at the beach.

I feel the happiness as a child again as the cool of the waves gently ebbs back and forth across and feet.

I feel the comfort of God upon me in the form of a gentle breeze that surrounds me, as I hear God whisper in my ear: "I love you today, now, and tomorrow, and even when there is no yesterday. I love you for all time."

I live, laugh, love, grow, and explore life, walking in love with my family until yesterday does not exist.

Whenever yesterday is in the past,
I remember how their love for me simply did not last.
For how could they love someone with problems they did not understand?
In their ignorance, they turned their love away.
They turned a blind eye to loving their sister, their daughter.

As long as I live in the land of yesterday,
I feel loved, safe, and happy.
But much to my misfortune, I cannot stay where I am loved in yesterday forever.
For yesterday turns into tomorrow,
And then yesterday ceases to exist.
The love of yesterday dwindles as hearts grow cold in ignorance and misunderstanding.
And love begins to cease to exist to disappear across time.
The brokenness of life is a great continuum.
Disappointment exists everywhere all of the time,
Just waiting to be realized by one more person.
When disappointment is realized by just one more person one more time—it is a thief!
Disappointment steals the joy, the little moments of happiness in all of your yesterdays, which slowly turn into yesteryears.

Then one day, yesterday is so far away, it's at the beginning of life, and you find yourself in life's final stages.

It is here when you begin to look for the moments disappointment stole in all of your yesteryears.

Oh! To steal these moments of joy back!

You long to experience the joy of yesteryears just one more time.

As time wastes away your body, you long to relive your favorite moments of joy in your yesteryears.

As you think on these moments, trying to regain your joy, it is then that you realize the only moments that disappointment cannot steal are the moments you had when you experienced God's love and enjoyed his company.

For Jesus Christ's love is the only love in existence that is perfect, and it never leaves you even when disappointment steals love, steals understanding, steals joy. It cannot steal the love of God because God is perfect, and God's perfect love cannot be stolen because it is ever present, everlasting, ever knowing, always existing.

His love is the same for you yesterday as it is today and tomorrow, which is greater than you can fathom.

So do not despair when life's disappointments steal, when your family turns their love away from you, for God is greater than all of life's problems and disappointments.

God loves in your moments of joy in your yesterdays, and he will continue to always love you throughout the pain even as you waste away until your body is no more. He never disappointments; his love is always the same and never changes.

God loves you in your yesterdays, todays, and tomorrows.

Content Reference Based on Poem's Themes

Comfort of God:

If you have any encouragement from being united with Christ, if any comfort from his love, if any fellowship with the Spirit, if any tenderness and compassion, then make my joy complete by being like-minded, having the same love, being one in spirit and purpose. Do nothing out of selfish ambition or vain conceit, but in humility consider others better than yourselves. Each of you should look not only to your own interests, but also to the interests of others. (Philippians 2:1–4 NIV)

NIV One Touch Bible Soft Computer Program, 2019, www.biblesoft.com

Jesus Christ's Perfect Love and God's Love:

But if anyone obeys his word, God's love is truly made complete in him. This is how we know we are in him: Whoever claims to live in him must walk as Jesus did. (1 John 2:5–6 NIV)

NIV One Touch Bible Soft Computer Program, 2019, www.biblesoft.com

And the Rocks Cried Out!

A pretty Victorian house sits on the shores and the rocky cliffs above.
Waves, sometimes clamorous, sometimes calm and peaceful, rock
and ebb on the rocky shore
    Below the home.
The yellow Victorian home is a part of modern art and poetry.
It tells the tales of the lives it once held so dear.
Like a gentle, cool summer night's breeze on the starless night that
passes by a full moon,
Poetry whispers many things into the years:
Of beauty, of love, of nature, of loss, of sadness, of serenity, of tall
tales and laughter gone past …
Poetry whispers.

The yellow Victorian home's wall's whisper some, the same things
that poetry whispers at night.
The home whispers through the ghosts of people who lived there in
the pasts or through the frustrations
    Of current owners muttering around the house.

More time goes by.
More time brings new stories to the home in life.
Life itself, nature around us, silently tells us more stories
As time goes past.

The cry of an eagle, the roar of a tiger, the sigh of contentment that
is carried by the wind across the
    Earth.
While contentment fills the earth's quiet unnoticeable places,
The sadness is what is most memorable about life on earth.

Sadness tells a story with evidence left behind in the Victorian home.
Monuments and graves are created every day to the tune to the same
poetic story we will all face one day: the
    sadness of loss of life, of loved ones.
We will all face our own death one day.
Is this true loss?
I think not!

The poetic sadness in death does death injustice to death itself.
For death is just a doorway,
Death is just a stepping stone
To a continuation of more life on the other side—
If you have eternal life in Jesus Christ.

The earth's greatest story that is most often ignored is this:
If you accept the free gift of the water of life, which is salvation
through Jesus Christ, then you will have
    eternal life in His name and go to heaven after you die.
You can accept the free gift of the water of life by genuinely asking
Jesus Christ into your heart and life
    To be your personal Lord and Savior of your life, and by asking
    Jesus Christ place your name in the Book of Life.
If you do this and mean it, then you will have salvation through
Jesus Christ.
If people will not proclaim the gospel, then who is willing?
If people will not praise God, then will not the rocks cry out?

As I stroll along the rocky cliff's outside edge in front of the yellow
Victorian home in front of the cliff, I
Look down, and I see the waves crashing clamorously against the
rocks along the shore.
From below, I hear whispers rising, praising God, and from behind
me, I hear the poetic whispers of the

past, of the stories of the people now dead who once lived in the Victorian home, and the story of how they witnessed for Christ when they were alive.

And the rocks cried out!

Scripture Reference Based on Quoted Scripture the Poem Is Based On

"I tell you," he replied, "if they keep quiet, the stones will cry out." (Luke 19:40 NIV)

NIV One Touch Bible Soft Computer Program, 2019, www. biblesoft.com

Section 4

Poems Related to Brokenness of Life, and Family Related to Christianity

The Pain of the Word Family and How to Correct It

Family.
I am forever haunted by the word: Family.
The word that I used to hold so dear.
The word that used to mean the world.
Now all the word does is remind me of the gaping hole in my heart.

It is a gaping hole—a wound that is too large to ever be closed.
It is a mortal wound to the soul.
Every time the word *family* is uttered, I am reminded of the gaping hole in my heart.

The gaping hole in my heart is the absence or the lack of what once was my family.
A time ago, hallways were filled with food, laughter, and rejoicing as we traveled to reunite with one
    another in the bonds of peace and love.
Slowly, religious differences drove a wedge between us, and I was thrown out into the cold.
After some time passed, I was forgiven and allowed back in.
During this time, I experienced the pain of separation and hell never to be allowed back in and
    never to be loved or accepted again because of my views on
    Christ.
But then came forgiveness.
Then I was graciously let back in.
I was so happy to be a part of my family once again.
But sadly, this would not last.

One day, another disagreement of a serious nature arose.

One thought I lied when I told the truth; another lied to get out of trouble.

The one who lied was the one who was believed, and that was all that mattered.

His lie cost me my relationship with this family member as well as my reputation.

It would have cost one of us in the end, either him or me.

He made sure it was me.

The only way I found I could forgive him for his heinous lie

Was never to utter the word *family* around him again.

Never to speak of any of my family members, and what goes on in their lives, with him ever again.

To be kept in the dark—oh, ignorant dismay!

It may seem like ignorant bliss!

But every time I hear him pray and utter the word *family*, it is like a knife twisting into my heart and

> soul, tearing the mortal spiritual wound open a little bit wider each time, making me a little bit further away from my family every time he says the word *family*.

Beware family quarrels and the need to forgive!

For both, you will find, may cost you big!

The pain of both is separation of one kind or another—a form of invisible isolation in order to move on.

> You cannot speak of the past or know of the future—a painful separation—while being ever present minded that the pain your disagreement caused you will always separate you from your loved ones; it forms the barrier of the word *family*.

Family is pain.

Family is disagreement.

Family is separation.

Families should never give up on each other, but all too often they do.

Will you survive the more you hear the word *family*, twist the knife, and murder your soul?

Only by the grace of God will you be made whole one day.

Then maybe *family* will have a new meaning.

A meaning that it should.

God's family has the meaning it should.

God's family—the body of Christ—accepts, loves, never gives up on you, and forgives.

When you lose your family on earth or feel the pain of the word *family*, look to God for a new family
> and to have the family the way it should be—hidden within the body of Christ.

Then Christ will take your pain away from you,

If you ask,

But it may not happen right away or in the way you expect,

And it will only happen if you believe it is granted to you by Christ.

Then you will receive Christ's comfort, Christ carrying your burdens for you on the cross.

And one day,

You will be excluded no more,

When you are welcomed home to heaven

In the body of Christ.

My hope lies in being welcomed into my new family as a full-fledged member of the body of Christ,
> never to be thrown away by family or excluded by family ever again.

Content Reference Based on Poem's Themes

God's Grace:

Each one should use whatever gift he has received to serve others, faithfully administering God's grace in its various forms. If anyone speaks, he should do it as one speaking the very words of God. If anyone serves, he should do it with the strength God provides, so that in all things God may be praised through Jesus Christ. To him be the glory and the power for ever and ever. Amen. (1 Peter 4:10–11 NIV)

NIV One Touch Bible Soft Computer Program, 2019, <u>www.biblesoft.com</u>

God's Acceptance, Love, and Forgiveness:

Here is a trustworthy saying that deserves full acceptance: Christ Jesus came into the world to save sinners—of whom I am the worst. 16 But for that very reason I was shown mercy so that in me, the worst of sinners, Christ Jesus might display his unlimited patience as an example for those who would believe on him and receive eternal life. (1 Timothy 1:15–16 NIV)

NIV One Touch Bible Soft Computer Program, 2019, <u>www.biblesoft.com</u>

"As the Father has loved me, so have I loved you. Now remain in my love. If you obey my commands, you will remain in my love, just as I have obeyed my Father's commands and remain in his love. I have told you this so that my joy may be in you and that your joy may be complete. My command is this: Love each other as I have loved you. Greater love has no one than this, that he lay down his life for his friends. You are my friends if you do what I command. I no longer call you servants, because a servant does not know his master's business. Instead, I have called you friends, for everything that I learned from my Father I have made known to you. You did not choose me, but I chose you and appointed you to go and bear fruit—fruit that will last. Then the Father will give you whatever you ask in my name. This is my command: Love each other. (John 15:9–17 NIV)

NIV One Touch Bible Soft Computer Program, 2019, <u>www.</u><u>biblesoft.com</u>

Lord and may please him in every way: bearing fruit in every good work, growing in the knowledge of God, being strengthened with all power according to his glorious might so that you may have great endurance and patience, and joyfully giving thanks to the Father, who has qualified you to share in the inheritance of the saints in the kingdom of light. For he has rescued us from the dominion of darkness and brought us into the kingdom of the Son he loves, in whom we have redemption, the forgiveness of sins. (Colossians 1:10–14 NIV)

NIV One Touch Bible Soft Computer Program, 2019, <u>www.</u><u>biblesoft.com</u>

Christ Carries Our Burdens for Us

Praise be to the Lord, to God our Savior, who daily bears our burdens. (Psalm 68:19 NIV)

NIV One Touch Bible Soft Computer Program, 2019, <u>www.</u><u>biblesoft.com</u>

Lulling to Sleep on an Ocean of Broken Dreams

I live in a vast ocean,
Ever drowning in its never forgotten, lost sea,
Yet never really drowning in the face of reality.

I cannot be identified.
I have no body to speak of but only awareness.
I have a sense of spirit about me.
I live on the surface of the ocean.

Life is like the ocean.
My awareness, although my body does not appear to exist,
My awareness is my body.
As I live on the surface on the ocean,
I float through life.

Does this kind of life seem so easy?
Ah! That it can! But looks can be deceiving!
For rough seas can strike at a moment's notice!
And seas that are not rough are hidden with broken waves.

The broken waves carry many things that can turn into rough seas indeed!
They carry things that seem so easy and float by, like dreams that are born.
When born, they float along for a while.
These dreams rock you to sleep at night in your ocean called life.

Then one night, you have nightmares—oh, rough seas and winds too!

And you wake up only to realize sadness and disappointments.
Yes! Disappointments in life, the little ripples that were on your claim waves, creep in, and they
Slowly cause an undertow.
This undertow would pull you under and drowns you in despair one day if your dreams be destroyed you thought in dismay!
Yet time proved you wrong!
You learned to get along with the ocean.

A dance of drifting and floating, and some tumbling too!
You survived the loss of your dreams.
All the while, you were too painfully aware of your awareness in life—your ocean.

Then one day, you became aware as the warm sunshine shone down upon you.
God never disappoints when life does.
God uses your broken dreams, your broken heart, life's disappointments, life's broken dreams to somehow help others who are struggling.
"How?" you ask.
The key is you!
As you float, toss, and tumble in your ocean and meet others along the way,
Be sure to learn from your failures, your successes, your disappointments, your struggles, your broken dreams. And be sure that whatever you can take away that is positive from it,
Whatever piece of driftwood that floats your way,
Whatever your life line that God provided you with,
Share it with others.

It might make all the difference in their lives.
It may be exactly what they need to hear.

It might speak words of life to them, words of peace to them, words of hope to them, words of encouragement to them.
It may save their lives.

So consider yourself blessed next time you are disappointed.
Consider yourself lucky if you are hated for the kingdom of heaven in Christ's name, for great is your reward in heaven.
If you help just one other person in this life with one single kind word that made a difference in one day of their lives,
Then you have already served a great purpose for God in this earth
And can do so much more,
The more you help others
As much as you can.

So learn to float with the ocean.
Learn to drift with the driftwood.
Learn to weather the storms at seas while rejoicing.
And remember to give thanks for your awareness in life.
And I know this can be hard,
Especially when you feel so small and insignificant,
So thrown away
And unloved.

If you can only take away one message, take away this: If everyone in this world throws you away, and you accept Jesus Christ, Jesus will always welcome you, will always completely love you for who you are, and will never throw you away. You will always be someone in Jesus's eyes, and you will always have a friend in Jesus.

So after having reflected on all of this in my awareness,
I float by calmly in my ocean,
Being rocked to sleep by its subtle waves,
No longer afraid of all my many disappointments
And the fact that all my dreams in life were shattered and broken.

Now I can drift on the ocean lulling to sleep,
And I never have to worry about never being someone in the world's eyes.
I am always someone in Jesus's eyes.
That is all that matters.

Content Scripture Reference Based on Poem's Themes

Being Hated for the Kingdom of God:

"If the world hates you, keep in mind that it hated me first. If you belonged to the world, it would love you as its own. As it is, you do not belong to the world, but I have chosen you out of the world. That is why the world hates you. (John 15:18–19 NIV)

NIV One Touch Bible Soft Computer Program, 2019, www. biblesoft.com

Jesus Deserves Our Acceptance:

Here is a trustworthy saying that deserves full acceptance: Christ Jesus came into the world to save sinners — of whom I am the worst. But for that very reason I was shown mercy so that in me, the worst of sinners, Christ Jesus might display his unlimited patience as an example for those who would believe on him and receive eternal life. Now to the King eternal, immortal, invisible, the only God, be honor and glory for ever and ever. Amen. (1 Timothy 1:15–17 NIV)

Important about Jesus:

The important thing is that in every way, whether from false motives or true, Christ is preached. And because of this I rejoice. (Philippians 1:18 NIV)

NIV One Touch Bible Soft Computer Program, 2019, www. biblesoft.com

If Only I Could Remain
in the Land of Before

Fractured at the heart,
Fractured in my mind,
My family decided one to cut me out of their lives.

Through turmoil and disagreements,
Beyond comprehension
Of why we all simply could not
All continue to get along,
To continue to carry on
And be a part of one another's lives.

Now apart,
We have become
A fractured family.

I often think of my fractured family,
My broken home.
Mistreated and misjudged,
Left behind and doomed to be forgotten by my family.

I try my best to remember the ones who threw me out.
I remember them and honor who I knew them to be,
Before we all began to disagree.

For disagreements cannot change love if it is true.
And the truth of the matter is this:
Though they turned their backs on me forever, I still love them.

I play records of their favorite childhood tunes
While looking at collages of recent and distant past times
That we shared that were happy,
While we all got along.

In sadness, I remember them in love,
Staring at the collages,
The good now tainted with sadness,
For there will be no new memories.
All I have left is what is past that was good.

As time distances itself between me and them,
I will be able to connect with them less and less,
Even if I remember what they like and who they were,
For time changes everyone.

While time may change them,
Their sentence against me is final.
I scream and cry as I look at the collages.
"No!" I think helplessly.
How will I ever get by?
The answer is simple.
I'll survive on grace.
Though I am excluded now,
God will not exclude me from heaven.

In sadness, I go forth into exile,
Remembering them by playing their favorite music every day,
Remembering them by looking at collages of happy times gone past,
And trying to hold on to what exists somewhere in time that was
good,
But only now exists somewhere caught up in time,
Caught up in the past,
Caught up in what was.

As I cry myself to sleep every night,
Wishing things were different
And gaining the strength to survive
Only when I need it most,
Because God pulls through for me always
When I need him most.

As I drift off to sleep
And dream peaceful dreams
Of a home full of laughter,
Newness of life,
Good memories of the past as they were forming.

And only in my dreams
Can I exist in somewhere in time
Alongside my family
As if nothing ever happened.
It is here I can exist again
with my family that threw me away.
Laughing with them and loving others again,
Untainted by life,
Once again.

And when I need a break from reliving the good times,
Somewhere in my mind, in dreams,
Somewhere in time,
I wake up within the dream,
And I find myself floating peacefully on a raft,
In a sea that is impossible to drown in,
For it does not really exist
Except in my mind.
I rock back and forth
Peacefully on the raft
And fall asleep again,

With the sun beating down on me.

And I am with my family once again,
And we aren't fractured anymore,
Because it's a dream.
It's before it really happened.
We are all loving each other and enjoying one another
As we were never able to do so well.
We are in life.
We are in the past.

Sometimes life causes so much pain.
If only we still welcomed each other—
That is all I regret:
Not what I said to them,
Only that they chose to walk away.
For in what I said, I said out of love, a concern,
Which they took the wrong way,
Dismissing me forever
And throwing me away.

Why can we not act as brothers and sisters should?
If only I could go back and live.
Ah, yes!
I can go back and live
In the land of before.
When I place myself in the past
And I dream of what once was,
Then I am dwelling in the land of before.

It is here, in the land of before,
That I will never miss seeing my family, for their memories are alive,
And they will never leave me.
Because the future, in which they discarded me,

Will never occur,
For the future never comes
In the land of before.
Only the past, frozen in segments of time,
Exists in the land of before.

If I live in my dreams,
Then I am dwelling in the land of before.
So every night,
I dream of my family
And our past, good memories.
I escape the present,
And I tarry just a little while,
Caught up
Somewhere in time,
In the land of before.

Content Reference Based on Poem's Themes

God's Grace:

Each one should use whatever gift he has received to serve others, faithfully administering God's grace in its various forms. If anyone speaks, he should do it as one speaking the very words of God. If anyone serves, he should do it with the strength God provides, so that in all things God may be praised through Jesus Christ. To him be the glory and the power for ever and ever. Amen. (1 Peter 4:10–11 NIV)

NIV One Touch Bible Soft Computer Program, 2019, www.biblesoft.com

Beware! And Be Sure Never to Enter the Garden of Possibilities

A world full of sadness and pain
Is hidden deep within my heart
Because some of my family members chose to walk away.

They walked away from my life.
They dismissed me forever,
Never to forgive me over misunderstandings and disagreements
taken the wrong way.

Now out of my life,
I am left with good memories that are in the past.
I know what I can do to make what ceases to exist last
Instead of letting time erase all memories of how my family was in
life, because time distances me the
 longer I am out of their lives.
I'll dwell in my mind
And let my mind create scenes of joy, laughter, fun, scenes of all of
sharing together again!
In a scene of beauty that is constantly morphing into more beautifully
memories of them,
Memories of them that don't really exist,
Memories of them that exist only in my mind,
In a beautiful garden of possibilities.

Any good thing could happen to these memories,
Always forming, always changing into something better than the
previous memory.
In the garden of possibilities,

These memories are all beautiful.
They are all of what could be,
Not of what actually was,
So they do not really exist
Except as a hope, a dream, a vision inside my head,
And they exist in the realm of possibilities.

So I'll close my eyes,
And I'll let these beautiful memories take over my mind forever,
Making my mind a delightful, inhabitable place of wonderment
and possibility,
The possibility that no pain they actually inflicted in life will ever
hurt me,
For pain does not exist in a land of a beautiful garden of possibilities.

Then one day when I get tired of dwelling in beauty of the land of
possibilities,
I'll wake up and remind myself from my beautiful dream that
These visions and dreams were what I wanted to be, not what
actually was,
They were only what I wished would happen,
And not actually what would ever be.

There is another name for the garden of possibilities: the land of
what could be.
In the land of what could be, people tend to shut out negativity in
all of its forms.
These negative memories with your loved ones who threw you away
will be ignored if they existed in
    reality or perhaps forgotten,
But in the land of what could be, they will never exist.
These memories of pain will never be because they are not beautiful.
Neither will the pain from the sin that would come from the actual
memory from real life's imperfect

scene of reality played out, because to remember the sin is to remember or relive your pain,
which only makes the pain of being cast aside worse.
But as long as I choose to tarry in the garden of possibilities of memories that are creating what could be,
In a land that could be:
I'll find beauty,
I'll find rest,
I'll escape perhaps in my mind for just a little while,
And in doing so think of my family members in love.
And the pain they caused me by throwing me out won't hurt quite as much as long as I focus on something positive about them, even if it ceases to exist.
It ever existed, and it is positive.
Cling to all that is good,
Stay on the straight and narrow,
And face your fears
By leaving the sanctity of the garden of possibilities.
And when you do,
You'll have courage,
You'll be a better stronger person.
The secret to doing so successfully
Is asking and receiving all the grace you possibly can from God
And trusting that He will provide it in the moments you need it most.
Then, when the garden of possibilities is far into your distant past,
You'll feel good that you overcame, because God overcame the hardest thing you could go through in life:
Living through exclusion, and the process of being unloved.
So does anyone need to tarry in the garden of possibilities?
When pain is at its highest,
They may rest here for a little while,
When they accept the greater help from God to get back on their feet

And have strength they can't identify its origin carrying their footsteps so they don't make a sound.

If you choose to let God's grace carry you,

You will not need to tarry in the garden of possibilities.

You may not need to even visit the garden of possibilities if you focus your attention on God instead of letting your pain carry you.

People's folly is that they enter the garden of possibilities when their pain is at its peak because they let their pain carry them, instead of letting God carry them all the way through the rest of their lives.

The problems you face and overcome with God's help while God carries you is no easy task, but it's the only way to survive.

So beware the next time you desire to enter the garden of possibilities, and for your own good,

Let God carry you. Never, enter to the garden of possibilities to begin with, and things will go

    better for you in the long run!

Content Reference Based on Poem's Themes

God's Grace:

Each one should use whatever gift he has received to serve others, faithfully administering God's grace in its various forms. If anyone speaks, he should do it as one speaking the very words of God. If anyone serves, he should do it with the strength God provides, so that in all things God may be praised through Jesus Christ. To him be the glory and the power for ever and ever. Amen. (1 Peter 4:10–11 NIV)

NIV One Touch Bible Soft Computer Program, 2019, www. biblesoft.com

God Carries Your Burdens:

Praise be to the Lord, to God our Savior, who daily bears our burdens. (Psalm 68:19 NIV)

NIV One Touch Bible Soft Computer Program, 2019, www. biblesoft.com

Overcomer in Christ:

Yet you have a few people in Sardis who have not soiled their clothes. They will walk with me, dressed in white, for they are worthy. He who overcomes will, like them, be dressed in white. I will never blot out his name from the book of life, but will acknowledge his name before my Father and his angels. Whoever has ears, let them hear what the Spirit says to the churches. (Revelation: 3:4–6 NIV)

NIV One Touch Bible Soft Computer Program, 2019, www. biblesoft.com

Section 5

Poems Dealing with Faith in God and Christianity

A Lullaby of Peace Finds the Nations!

It floats on the air,
Calmly rocking back and forth.
The gentle breezes lullaby.
The warm sunshine makes peace more radiant,
    More transparent!
As God's redemption makes us more acceptable to enter
    Into the kingdom of heaven,
The dove is a messenger of peace and redemption of the nations!
She carries the olive branch in her mouth across the distant shores,
Offering it to each and every nation!
Oh, which nation will accept peace?
Which among the nations will receive Christ's redemption
And wash their robes so that they are clean and have been made pure
and acceptable again?
Who will choose to wash away their disgrace and war?
When a nation does, it will be like the dove.
The dove—whose blue deep eyes are pools,
Yes! Pools of tears, an expression that the nation's sins, contained by
the peace of the dove.
Soon their sins will hurt no more!
Covered in transparency, the brilliant white robes of righteousness
remind of the feathers of the dove.
God provides both, and both are made acceptable!
In grace, the dove carries her message, her olive branch,
Flying above the beach,
Searching for the perfect place to lay down her branch!
One day, God shows her where to lay her branch down, and so
She lands!

As graceful a sight as can be!
She follows God's orders and lays down her branch!
Now peace will follow this chosen nation where God showed her where to lay down the branch.
It is here,
In the land for all the nations to see for all time!

Scripture Reference Based on Quoted Scripture the Poem Is Based On

Blessed are those who wash their robes, that they may have the right to the tree of life and may go through the gates into the city. (Revelation 22:14 NIV)

NIV One Touch Bible Soft Computer Program, 2019, www. biblesoft.com

How to Come to Faith: Oh, Where Does My Faith Begin?

Faith is a seed planted in your heart by God.

Faith starts with belief to the testimony that Jesus Christ is who he says he is,

 And the Bible is the complete truth inspired by God.

The Bible is God's word.

You come to believe by hearing, believing, and understanding God's word, and how to put it to practice—that is how to live for Christ.

The more you learn about Christ's love and what he gave—his life so that your soul would go to heaven to live with him after you die—the more you begin to believe.

The more you begin to believe, the more your heart opens.

Oh! To drink of Christ's love! It makes your heart desire the free gift of the water of life!

The free gift of the water of life is a self-sustaining joy—found in the secret place, which is your heart, and it is eternal!

Oh, to drink of this joy—the joy of salvation—is to overcome!

You overcome because Christ overcame spiritual death, which is the second death, or hell, for you!

He wants abundant life for everyone!

Abundant life is true life! A life to the full of love for Christ, and everyone it is life that satisfies your thirst, for if you drink of the abundant life of Christ, you drink of the free gift of the water of life and have salvation in Christ!

So if you are willing, come and drink of the free gift of the water of life!

Believe the testimony of the Holy Spirit that Jesus Christ had on this earth, who is part of Yahweh's Spirit!

The Holy Spirit will testify to you that Jesus Christ is the way, the truth, and the life, and that no one comes to the Father except through Jesus Christ.

The Holy Spirit is a living testimony that Jesus Christ is who he says he is, and that Jesus Christ did in fact die for the sins of the world, and was raised for your justification! Accept and believe! today, Not tomorrow, before it is too late!

For if you wait to accept the gift, then you may die, and it may be too late to accept, and a place of eternal torment and punishment for your sins, for you would not have forgiveness without salvation and therefore will not have justification if you are not saved!

So how do you recognize this testimony that the Holy Spirit brings to you?

By experiencing the Holy Spirit through prayer in the way the Bible teaches.

If you cannot discern if the Holy Spirit is among your midst when you pray, I'll tell you how to discern in a few ways.

Four ways to recognize the Holy Spirit during prayer, I will tell you. First, it takes prayer like in the gospel of Matthew, where two or more or gathered—here am I, Jesus tells us.

You can experience Jesus Christ by experiencing the Holy Spirit in prayer—first by praying with at least two people together so that Jesus will be in your midst!

The second thing I'll reveal to you is this: If one of the person's praying with you has the Holy Spirit living with them and in them always, and they pray for healing by laying on of hands—if their hands heat up or radiate heat out of their hands form within themselves while they pray for you, the Holy Spirit is present!

Thirdly, if neither of you have the Holy Spirit but you want him to be present, let two or more of you together pray in faith, believing that the Holy Spirit is real and the truth; invite him to be in your midst, and he will answer you!

The fourth thing I'll tell you is this: When you experience the healing heat or a quiet peace that overshadows you—a peace you can't explain or describe, a peace that surpasses all understanding and reasoning—the Holy Spirit is in your midst! His peace is comforting you!

While there are other ways to experience God and his Spirit— the Holy Spirit, in addition to these four things—when you have experienced the things I just described, you have experienced the Holy Spirit.

Finally, friends, when you experience the Holy Spirit and believe within your heart—which is the secret place—that Jesus Christ died for the sins of the world, and was raised from the dead so that we could have eternal life in Jesus Christ's name, you will have eternal life in Jesus Christ's name when you invite Jesus Christ to come and live in your heart and be with you and in you always; you believed because of the Holy Spirit, and you received Jesus Christ into your heart.

In welcoming Jesus Christ into your heart and life, to rule over you, I'll tell you a little secret: You welcomed the Holy Spirit too!

Scripture Reference Based on Quoted Scripture the Poem Is Based On

The Spirit and the bride say, "Come!" And let him who hears say, "Come!" Whoever is thirsty, let him come; and whoever wishes, let him take the free gift of the water of life. (Revelation 22:17 NIV)

NIV One Touch Bible Soft Computer Program, 2019, www. biblesoft.com

Therefore I tell you that no one who is speaking by the Spirit of God says, "Jesus be cursed," and no one can say, "Jesus is Lord," except by the Holy Spirit. (1 Corinthians 12:3 NIV)

NIV One Touch Bible Soft Computer Program, 2019, www. biblesoft.com

"Again, I tell you that if two of you on earth agree about anything you ask for, it will be done for you by my Father in heaven. For where two or three come together in my name, there am I with them." (Matthew 18:19–20 NIV)

NIV One Touch Bible Soft Computer Program, 2019, <u>www.biblesoft.com</u>

And I will ask the Father, and he will give you another Counselor to be with you forever—the Spirit of truth. The world cannot accept him, because it neither sees him nor knows him. But you know him, for he lives with you and will be in you. I will not leave you as orphans; I will come to you. (John 14:16–18 NIV)

NIV One Touch Bible Soft Computer Program, 2019, <u>www.biblesoft.com</u>

The Unknown Hypocrite

Once there was an unknown hypocrite.
He dwelled in an average city and had a good job.
He was loved by all of his peers.

He peers did not realize that they did not really know the man they thought they loved.
The man they thought they loved was really an unknown hypocrite.
This man did not realize that he was a hypocrite in his way because he could not recognize his own sin.
He could not recognize his own sin, the log in his eye, because he always tried to minimize his sin, or
> cover it up by hiding it from the eyes of the ever-watchful world of those who loved him.
This hypocrite was unknown because he did not realize that he was a hypocrite as he walked
> throughout the course of his life.
Like the hypocrites of Jesus's time, the Pharisees, he loved to pray in public.
He always made an excuse when he prayed in public with his family that it was not for show, yet everybody could tell that he was praying when he did.
He would bow his head, and it would be obvious that he appeared pious to the world in these moments.
He lived life encouraging others to do the same, to pray in public not matter what others thought, and insisted that it was not for show, yet it was always on display.
He wore religious symbols and went around with Bibles.
He made a big to-do about repenting.

He did not realize that by gathering around his relatives when he wanted to appear to repent, that was all he was doing—making a big show and *appearing* to repent.

Appearances are all that matter to hypocrites.

Hypocrites come in all shapes and sizes and are from all backgrounds in society.

He would make rules on how people would hold him accountable to repent for when he messed up.

Sadly, he did not realize this meant he would already not be successful in repenting, because this was the

wrong approach to true repentance.

The Bible tells us to "turn away from our sins" and "go and sin no more."

What the man did not realize was that it is possible to repent overnight, and go and sin no more—a clean

break from the behavior he truly desired to stop.

It would take asking Jesus Christ in secret to do the impossible for him and to believe that the impossible was done for him—that he would have 100 percent victory in what he desired to repent of.

Next, it would take turning his mind and heart over to God and praying when temptation struck.

This man did not realize that he did not need other people to tell him when he was sinning so that he would stop.

This does not describe success.

His success would only come from within himself, when he relied on Jesus Christ and the Holy Spirit that he sent to help him—trusting God completely to overcome for him.

The hypocrite continued to make donations to organizations, although not readily apparent, which was to his merit.

But praying in public in such a way that everyone around you knows you are praying is for show, even if you say it's not, and making a big deal about repenting of something in front of others, setting boundaries and giving rules like it's a game to the man, is also hypocrisy and therefore evil.

Be accountable to God.

Trust God to give you success in repentance.

When you pray in public, do it in such a way that people don't know you are praying.

When you donate, do it anonymously so that no one knows who gave.

These are all ways to fight the hypocrisy of today.

Be warned to guard your heart, your mind, and your actions so that you do nothing that can be perceived as religious and seen by others and things will go better for you.

Do this, and you will never have to find out one day that you were that unknown hypocrite, lying to yourself about your actions and doing everything where everyone could see it.

Never let your right hand know what your left hand is doing, and things will go well with you.

Take heed to the things I've said you can do to fight hypocrisy.

Start living for God

And working for God in secret.

Then you will never be an unknown hypocrite,

And great in heaven your reward will be!

Scripture Reference Based on Quoted Scripture the Poem Is Based On

"No one, sir," she said. "Then neither do I condemn you," Jesus declared. "Go now and leave your life of sin." (John 8:11 NIV)

NIV One Touch Bible Soft Computer Program, 2019, www.biblesoft.com

Matthew 6:33

But seek first his kingdom and his righteousness, and all these things will be given to you as well. (Matthew 6:33 NIV)

NIV One Touch Bible Soft Computer Program, 2019, www.biblesoft.com

Content Reference Based on Poem's Themes

Jesus Declares the Pharisees Hypocrites:

Then Jesus said to the crowds and to his disciples: "The teachers of the law and the Pharisees sit in Moses' seat. So you must obey them and do everything they tell you. But do not do what they do, for they do not practice what they preach. They tie up heavy loads and put them on men's shoulders, but they themselves are not willing to lift a finger to move them.

"Everything they do is done for men to see: They make their phylacteries wide and the tassels on their garments long; they love the place of honor at banquets and the most important seats in the synagogues; they love to be greeted in the marketplaces and to have men call them 'Rabbi.'

"But you are not to be called 'Rabbi,' for you have only one Master and you are all brothers. And do not call anyone on earth 'father,' for you have one Father, and he is in heaven. Nor are you to be called 'teacher,' for you have one Teacher, the Christ. The greatest among you will be your servant. For whoever exalts himself will be humbled, and whoever humbles himself will be exalted.

"Woe to you, teachers of the law and Pharisees, you hypocrites! You shut the kingdom of heaven in men's faces. You yourselves do not enter, nor will you let those enter who are trying to.

"Woe to you, teachers of the law and Pharisees, you hypocrites! You travel over land and sea to win a single convert, and when he becomes one, you make him twice as much a son of hell as you are." (Matthew 23:1–15 NIV)

NIV One Touch Bible Soft Computer Program, 2019, www. biblesoft.com

How to Stand Firm, You Faith!

Stand firm, you faith!
I hold so dear!
If I cannot firmly believe
In Jesus Christ
Having died for my justification
And being raised for my redemption,
Then I have nothing left after I die except eternal torment.

If I do not accept the gift,
Which is called the free gift of the water of life,
By faith you believed
That Jesus Christ was the truth
Because the Holy Spirit came
And ministered to me in the way
That the Bible said he would.
A living testimony that Jesus Christ—he is Lord and King, forever!
A living word, alive and always true,
To be experienced throughout our daily lives
As the Holy Spirit ministers to us,
As the Holy Spirit that Jesus Christ sent intercedes
    On our behalf.
Our faith—our foggy mirror in this life begins to become clear.
The stronger our faith—the more clearly we see
The truth of the gospel, and about salvation.
The truth of gospel stands the test of time,
Inspired by God,
Who cannot tell a lie.
The stronger our faith, the clearer we see

That salvation starts with belief,
But it is our faith that saves us
Through the grace of God,
Meeting our every need,
Getting us through each day.
Helping us grow and learn about his ways.
The Holy Spirit that Jesus Christ sent,
When received in a greater measure with anointing by oil,
Will be so intimately close to us,
Within us, and with us always and forever.

We learn to listen to God's voice
And know who he is.
A secret blessing, a true gift from God, and a Holy calling in life,
This anointing with oil,
To do the work the Holy Spirit that Jesus Christ sent gave you to
do in this life,
Not to be mocked or taken lightly.
When we receive the Holy Spirit
And we learn to recognize him,
Interacting with us,
We learn to hear God's voice.
It is the voice of truth,
God cannot lie to us.
When we learn to recognize his voice,
We know we have him,
And on that day, we can rejoice,
As we do his work,
For the Holy Spirit is a deposit guaranteeing our salvation!

So if you question how to have salvation, just know
If you truly have the Holy Spirit that Jesus Christ sent,
You have salvation.
You desire the gift of salvation in your heart,

A desire placed on your heart by the Holy Spirit in the secret place within yourself.
So you ask God for his gift
So that you can have salvation
And thereby drink of the free gift of the water of life offered to all.
Finally, know that you are saved by your faith through grace so that no man can boast.

Scripture Reference Based on Quoted Scripture the Poem Is Based On

The Spirit and Bride say, "Come!" and let him who hear say, "Come!" whoever is thirsty, let him come; and whoever wishes, let him take the free gift of the water of life. (Revelation 22:17 NIV)

NIV One Touch Bible Soft Computer Program, 2019, www. biblesoft.com

It is impossible for those who have once been enlightened, who have tasted the heavenly gift, who have shared in the Holy Spirit, who have tasted the goodness of the word of God and the powers of the coming age, if they fall away, to be brought back to repentance, because to their loss they are crucifying the Son of God all over again and subjecting him to public disgrace. (Hebrews 6:4–6 NIV)

NIV One Touch Bible Soft Computer Program, 2019, www. biblesoft.com

For it is by grace you have been saved, through faith—and this not from yourselves, it is the gift of God—not by works, so that no one can boast. (Ephesians 2:8–9 NIV)

NIV One Touch Bible Soft Computer Program, 2019, www. biblesoft.com

Section 6

Words That Speak Life in Voluntary Institutions Other Than Jail

A Friend I'd Like to Have

Throughout the world, there are many people.
Some are trustworthy,
Some are loyal,
Some are true to themselves.

But in the world, there lurks a type of friend that no one understands.
A type of friend who was once untrustworthy and true,
A friend who was once a liar and a thief,
A friend who is just learning how to be a better person,
A friend who is learning to be just like me and you.

This person took too many wrong turns in their lives,
But everyone deserves a second chance.
And no matter how many bad things they have done,
God is willing to save them.
God calls everyone to repentance.
No matter how wretched this person is,
God loves them too, just like you and me.

Remember that no matter what one's sins are,
No one is better than anyone else.
For many people keep their secret sins,
Hidden in the dark,
And parade around as good people
With not much bad going on in their lives.
They have good lives,
And no one notices their sins.
But God notices their sins
And knows all of them.

He calls us to forgiveness—to forgive each other all our wrongs.
He calls us to repentance, to turn away from our sins,
Whether they are exposed in the light in life or not.
God is always calling us to change and be a better person.

The friend I'd like to have is the one who messed up big
And is determined to repent of what they did.
They are determined to get victory in Christ over their sins,
They are determined to change,
And they are truly sorry for what they did.
This is the type of person who has more character than all of the
ones whose sins remain hidden until judgment day,
For they are the ones who will succeed and gain victory over their
sins
As long as they rely on God to do the impossible for them.
Someone who is open to change and sorry for their sins
Is a true friend through and through,
For they are the sinner who wants to repent, and wants God and
salvation too.
And if they search for it like gold, they will find what they are
looking for
And be truly happy when they see their successes in hindsight.
And if they mess up once again,
God stands ready to forgive
And help them every step of the way to repent of their sins—
Every time.
God never fails us even when we fail ourselves.
God never leaves or forsakes us for all time, once we have him as
savior and receive the Holy Spirit.

Scripture Reference Based on Quoted Scripture the Poem Is Based On

Therefore I tell you that no one who is speaking by the Spirit of God says, "Jesus be cursed," and no one can say, "Jesus is Lord," except by the Holy Spirit. (1 Corinthians 12:3 NIV)

NIV One Touch Bible Soft Computer Program, 2019, www.biblesoft.com

Content Reference Based on Poem's Themes

Repentance:

I have not come to call the righteous, but sinners to repentance. (Luke 5:32 NIV)

NIV One Touch Bible Soft Computer Program, 2019, www.biblesoft.com

Forgiveness:

In him we have redemption through his blood, the forgiveness of sins, in accordance with the riches of God's grace that he lavished on us with all wisdom and understanding. He made know the mystery of his will according to his good pleasure, which he purposed in Christ. (Ephesians 1:7–9 NIV)

NIV One Touch Bible Soft Computer Program, 2019, www.biblesoft.com

Victory:

"Death has been swallowed up in victory." "Where, O death, is your victory? Where, O death, is your sting?" The sting of death is sin, and the power of sin is the law. But thanks be to God! He gives us the victory through our Lord Jesus Christ. (1 Corinthians 15:54–57 NIV)

NIV One Touch Bible Soft Computer Program, 2019, www.biblesoft.com

Find Your Ray of Hope, and Truly Live!

No one notices the last ray or sunlight disappearing as the sun goes down for the evening.

No one notices even the first bit of darkness that has crept in at night.

But after a while,

Everyone notices the darkness as it settles in,

Just as everyone notices the sunlight as it settles in for the day.

But remarkably,

Many notice the first ray sunlight to touch the ground at the start of a day.

Many people do not notice a single ray of sunshine peering through the clouds

As the afternoon rain ends.

But people always hold on to the first bit of hope that they notice,

That speaks to them,

That they can see that is real.

The real truth is that only someone amid sadness or despair

Will be the first one to notice hope

When it is truly here,

When it truly appears,

Whatever brought them hope.

Hope is like that first ray of sunlight in the morning,

But it is also like the ray that no one notices peering through the afternoon rain as it ends.

The only person to notice a hope this small is someone who is full of brokenness,

Full of despair.
Look for your ray of sunshine when you despair.
It may be hard to find,
But it is in front of you all or the time.
It was always there.
You simply have to learn to recognize your hope, your ray of sunshine,

And when you recognize,
Grab hold of it and never let it go.
And next time you are sad or despair,
Remember your ray of sunshine
And the way in which you took hold of it.

Oh! To have hope!
To have hope is to live!
To never find hope
Is the saddest person out there,
For without hope, they cannot find themselves, their calling, or
their future.
Seize hope
And live today!
Like every day is the first time you noticed your hope!
Let your hope that you took hold of renew your spirit!
And you will find fulfillment once you have hope and are renewed!

As for me,
My ray of hope is in Jesus Christ and the good news of his salvation,
My hope is in what the Holy Spirit gives me to do
And this life the Holy Spirit helps me get through.
Especially when I struggle,
I find
Hope, peace, and comfort in the Holy Spirit and what he does in
my life.

The most hope you can ever find is through Christ in Yahweh and
the Holy Spirit.
Where will you find your hope today?
When will you recognize your hope?
What does it look like for you?

Even if it is not what I described,
No matter what brings you simple hope, and even joy,
Give thanks to God for it
And know that the closer you get to Christ,
The closer you get to the Holy Spirit,
The closer you get to Yahweh,
And the more hope, and fulfillment you will find.
But it's the journey of a lifetime
To get to know who God really is!
Are you prepared for the journey?

If you are not,
Prepare your heart
By asking Jesus Christ into your heart to be your Savior
Out of the desire to be saved,
Which is placed in your heart because you believe.
You believe because you believe God's word is the truth,
You believe God,
And your belief is fortified when you experience the Holy Spirit
And know he is real.

When you experience the Holy Spirit,
You will know that Jesus Christ is Lord and who he said he is,
And that he still lives today!
You will find purpose in life by serving Jesus Christ
And letting the Holy Spirit
Show you what to do in life.

To initially receive the Holy Spirit in a small way,
First be sealed by the Father, Son, and Holy Spirit in baptism.
To receive the Holy Spirit in a mighty way,
Get your head anointed with oil
From someone who has the Holy Spirit.

And in the moments leading up to the anointing,
Invite the Holy Spirit
To be with you and in you always, to live and rest on you.

And the Holy Spirit will show you the way,
Will comfort you,
But not constantly.

The Holy Spirit, if you do God's will by being obedient to him,
Will help you know what to do in life
And give you a sense of purpose,
Although it may take a while to see that purpose.

It may take a while to notice your ray of sunshine peering through
the rain,
But the Holy Spirit was with you all the time through the whole
storm,
Never leaving you or forsaking you,
Always loving you.
For he is part of Yahweh's Spirit,
And like Jesus Christ, who loves you too,
He loves you dearly!

So make serving Christ your purpose today!
Hold on to Christ as your ray of sunshine,
Your ray of hope,
And let the Holy Spirit lead.
And far down the road,

You can look back
And say you were better for it,
And he gave you a new life
And a new hope.
And that there is abundant life
Out there,
Just waiting for you
To take hold of your sunshine!
Find it and treasure it
Today!
To treasure Christ in your heart—to belong to him—is to possess
the greatest treasure of all!
But remember it is Christ you belong to, and that he upholds you,
holds you so dear, and never lets you go!

Scripture Reference Based on Quoted Scripture the Poem Is Based On

And you also were included in Christ when you heard the word
of truth, the gospel of your salvation. Having believed, you were
marked in him with a seal, the promised Holy Spirit, who is a
deposit guaranteeing our inheritance until the redemption of those
who are God's possession—to the praise of his glory. (Ephesians
1:13–14 NIV)

NIV One Touch Bible Soft Computer Program, 2019, www.
biblesoft.com

John 14:3-4

And if I go and prepare a place for you, I will come back and take
you to be with me that you also may be where I am. You know the
way to the place where I am going. (John 14:3–4 NIV)

NIV One Touch Bible Soft Computer Program, 2019, www.biblesoft.com

For it is by grace you have been saved, through faith—and this not from yourselves, it is the gift of God—not by works, so that no one can boast. (Ephesians 2:8–9 NIV)

NIV One Touch Bible Soft Computer Program, 2019, www.biblesoft.com

Content Reference Based on Poem's Themes

How to Be Saved:

But what does it say? "The word is near you; it is in your mouth and in your heart," that is, the word of faith we are proclaiming: That if you confess with your mouth, "Jesus is Lord," and believe in your heart that God raised him from the dead, you will be saved. For it is with your heart that you believe and are justified, and it is with your mouth that you confess and are saved. As the Scripture says, "Anyone who trusts in him will never be put to shame." For there is no difference between Jew and Gentile — the same Lord is Lord of all and richly blesses all who call on him, for, "Everyone who calls on the name of the Lord will be saved." (Romans 10:8–13 NIV)

NIV One Touch Bible Soft Computer Program, 2019, www.biblesoft.com

John 6:37

All that the Father gives Me will come to Me, and the one who comes to Me I will by no means cast out. (John 6:37 NKJV)

NKJV One Touch Bible Soft Computer Program, 2019, www.biblesoft.com

God's Peace:

May the God of hope fill you with all joy and peace as you trust in him, so that you may overflow with hope by the power of the Holy Spirit. (Romans 15:13 NIV)

One Touch Bible Soft Computer Program, 2019, www.biblesoft.com

God Will Never Leave You or Forsake You:

And I will ask the Father, and he will give you another Counselor to be with you forever—the Spirit of truth. The world cannot accept him, because it neither sees him nor knows him. But you know him, for he lives with you and will be in you. I will not leave you as orphans; I will come to you. (John 14:16–18 NIV)

NIV One Touch Bible Soft Computer Program, 2019, www. biblesoft.com

Eternal Life in Jesus:

The Spirit gives life; the flesh counts for nothing. The words I have spoken to you are spirit and they are life. Yet there are some of you who do not believe. (John 6:63–64 NIV)

NIV One Touch Bible Soft Computer Program, 2019, www. biblesoft.com

Go through the Narrow Gate— When People Are Not Free the Path to Freedom

When people are not free, there is a secret path to freedom that most may never find.
The path is hidden within one's past
And is always left behind.
The key is in one's childhood;
It can be described in many ways.

It is the sense of wonder in all small and little things that occur throughout your day.
It is choosing to be happy when someone does something small that is nice for you.
Like giving you their piece of cake
When you are feeling sad and blue.
They have brightened your day
Through this simple action!
But it's not just in the act of giving!
It is hidden in the act of being kind by talking to others, and being grateful and accepting everything everyone does that is nice for you.
It is the act of enjoying everyone in conversation in every way that you can as best you can,
To heal, to mend, to brighten their day.
It is a selfless act of kindness you bring to others,
Not about what you can take for yourselves to feel better.

It is about stepping outside of your comfort zone.
It is about being the comfort to someone else

And not just about receiving comfort.
In being the comfort,
I'll tell you a little secret:
You'll feel a whole lot better,
And you will be comforted
Because you comforted others.

In being that comfort to someone else
In any way that you can,
By talking, by listening, by simply smiling,
By holding their hand and nodding encouragingly to let them know
you care,
To let them know you are here!

I'll tell you an even better secret:
There is someone who will always be with you and in you.
If you will accept him,
You may find comfort and a little peace too.

His name is the Holy Spirit.
He was sent by Jesus Christ.

You can receive him by inviting him to be with you and in you
always,
From within yourself silently,
And if your faith is strong
And you do not doubt,
He will answer you,
And come to you,
And live with you and in you always.

If you have the Holy Spirit in a greater measure in life,
He will comfort you, and he will help you.

You must always stand ready to ask God for forgiveness for your sins in any way you can,

Reaching out to him when you think you have sinned.

And if you feel pain upon your head, and you have received him,

It will go away.

You will experience his comfort through a cool mark, and his healing through a radiating heat upon your forehead;

He is doing some healing in your life.

Having the Holy Spirit rest on you in life

Is the greatest gift, comfort, and treasure you can receive!

It does not matter about your past sins in life;

If you ask forgiveness first,

All is well.

Another treasure is that the Holy Spirit will help you go home to Jesus Christ when you die;

He will carry you home, if you have him.

Even if he is not resting on you,

If you have salvation in Jesus's name, then Jesus Christ will come back for you.

I'll tell you a little secret: the Holy Spirit carrying you to heaven is Jesus's way of coming back for you.

But before you invite the Holy Spirit to come and rest on you,

Let's make sure you have salvation in Jesus Christ's name.

Invite Jesus Christ silently, within yourself, to come into your heart and be your savior,

To save you from going to hell, and to write your name in the book of life.

This ensures that you are saved first.

Then invite the Holy Spirit.

If you are able and have not, I urge you to get baptized.

Baptism is important.

You are saved by your faith, even if it's small and you lack confidence.

But you need to get baptized if you are able to do so and have not been.

If you have not been baptized and cannot get baptized, ask for salvation, and by the grace of Jesus Christ through your faith that you asked for the free gift of the water of life you will be saved.

Now rest and enjoy the comfort you will receive from the Holy Spirit if you invite him in!
If you do not choose to invite him,
At least choose to be that light in someone else's life
By smiling, by talking to them as you are able,
By encouraging them,
By holding their hand to let them know you care.
And by being selfless, giving them that piece of cake to cheer them up.
And be their comfort!
In being grateful for all of the little things you receive,
And in giving back to other's in the ways I just described,
You will be set free!
It is like entering the narrow gate;
It is like being a child again.
It was an experience left behind in childhood—the sense of satisfaction and wonder from receiving and giving from what others gave you, and what you did that was good for others.
I'll tell you a secret: If you walk in this way,
You are loving your neighbor,
Which God calls all of us to do.
If you walk in this way,
It will make you feel better about yourself
And give you a sense of satisfaction and a heightened sense of self-worth
That you have helped someone else in a way that you were able.
You have gladdened the heart of your neighbor.
You have given comfort
And received comfort.

And that is something
Everyone is capable of doing!
Now you are free again indeed!
Though you may not seem to be free,
You have found peace, and freedom,
So you are free indeed!

Scripture Reference Based on Quoted Scripture the Poem Is Based On

And I will ask the Father, and he will give you another Counselor to be with you forever—the Spirit of truth. The world cannot accept him, because it neither sees him nor knows him. But you know him, for he lives with you and will be in you. I will not leave you as orphans; I will come to you. (John 14:16–18 NIV)

NIV One Touch Bible Soft Computer Program, 2019, www. biblesoft.com

Shrouded in Darkness, You Are My Help

Shrouded in darkness
And full of despair.
Where is my help?
Where is my hope?

My hope is in Jesus Christ.
After I received him in an anointing, my greater help and comfort
came from the Holy Spirit, who was sent by Jesus Christ.
The Holy Spirit comes and comforts me with the cool mark on my
forehead.

As I lay in darkness, saddened, shrouded, broken, and crying,
God comforts me, and
I start to think of happier days, and
I smile at the memory of the smiles of those who love me.
I feel loved by God,
And I feel loved by all the smiling faces that once touched my life;
Some are still here, whereas others left by choice.
And even if they touched my life only for a moment in time,
I remember them, whether still a part of my life or now long gone,
by choice.
I remember the good, and I remember to give thanks to God
For all that I had in my life, have in my life. And I am just a little bit
more thankful for what God has given me each day, and
I wake up thanking God for what he gave me, with a newfound
appreciation for my life.

Content Reference Based on Poem's Themes

Hope:

Through him you believe in God, who raised him from the dead and glorified him, and so your faith and hope are in God. (1 Peter 1:21 NIV)

NIV One Touch Bible Soft Computer Program, 2019, www. biblesoft.com

Help and Comfort of God:

But you, O God, do see trouble and grief; you consider it to take it in hand. The victim commits himself to you; you are the helper of the fatherless. (Psalms 10:14 NIV)

NIV One Touch Bible Soft Computer Program, 2019, www. biblesoft.com

The Forgotten Ones (by Society)

Unbounded and unbroken,
We are the starving ones.
Forgotten and dismissed by society,
We try, we cry.
It is all in vain.

We have a few good days
While tucked away from society's grasp.
Our only major sins are our sicknesses.
Sunny days through the trees,
Peering, always peering.
The breeze causes the trees to wave to the breeze
As if to welcome the possibility of one more good, brand-new,
untarnished day.

Will today be happy or sad?
That depends on how we feel.
The attitude and boundaries are where it begins.
To have a good day, do what you can to make your day happy,
As long as it doesn't break any rules.

Once you're happy from playing ball in the warm sunshine
And laughing together, or coloring pictures for your family, whom
you miss while you are away,
You'll calm down and see that as long as you create a positive day,
you have the choice to make things.
Slowly get better as long as you deal with your sin, your sickness,
and other sinful interactions with others having a bad day in the
right way.
Will you let your sin win today?

These Are the Days That I Miss You

Warm sunshine on my face,
With gentle breezes giving me butterfly kisses upon my face.
I feel your love, your presence, although you are nowhere near.
I miss you and never forget the love I hunger for.
I miss your love, your presence, Mom.

I play in the yard that holds me captive—my love and sadness together.
As I play in the yard of sadness with new friends who are just passing through my life,
I enjoy the presence of my new friends for who they are.
For they will always be my friends and neighbors,
Even though they are just passing by.

And I remember my love for you, Mom.
It is hidden in the breeze that kisses my tears goodnight
While my new friends slowly pass me by in the night and move out of my life for good.
My tears upon my face at night, when I lay down to sleep, are your hugging and kissing me
Goodnight.

Content Reference Based on Poem's Themes

Love Your Neighbor as Yourself:

Jesus replied: "'Love the Lord your God with all your heart and with all your soul and with all your mind.' This is the first and greatest commandment. And the second is like it: 'Love your neighbor as yourself.' All the Law and the Prophets hang on these two commandments." (Matthew 22:37–40 NIV)

NIV One Touch Bible Soft Computer Program, 2019, www. biblesoft.com

Section 7

Poems Where You See Life

Holding on to Happiness

Warm sunshine, happy hippos, pink Frisbees whirling by.
I take refuge in the happiness of summertime.
People playing on the beach,
Escape to the coast,
Waves crashing on the jagged rocks.
A rainy day—
Will happiness be chased away?

No, happiness won't be chased away!
For happiness takes refuge in small, everyday delights!
Whatever brings a moment's joy,
A smile to your face.
Whatever gladdens your heart,
Cheers you up when you are brokenhearted.
Then happiness begins to find its way
Back into your heart that day!

Whatever form it may take,
It is different for everyone.
What makes your emotions run high
But bubble over with delight.
Whatever puts
Words and feelings you can't quite describe,
Because of the complexity of your happiness.
Then happiness has found you.

Happier times,
Good memories,
Dining with friends.

Holding fast to what makes life living, good, whole, pure, exciting, and worthwhile.
Remember to cling to these thoughts, feelings, memories, and objects that make you think of life as happy and worthwhile,
And life will start to go by faster.
You will be happier as time goes by
Because you will only see the good.
Even amid a rainy day, when people are hurting,
You will be the only one noticing and dearly holding on to
The single ray of sunshine that peers through the clouds,
That gives you a better hope
For a sunnier day,
Both today
And tomorrow.

The Monarch Butterfly Whose Death Is Never Seen

The monarch butterfly soars high into the skies.
He flies around the garden,
Resting on all the flowers.
He sees nothing but life and beauty all around.

The butterfly is full of beauty in himself.
Each butterfly has its own form of beauty unique to its own species.
They are like the essence of beauty and the beginning of spring as
they fly around.
They bring out everyone's inner child.

Everyone wants to chase.
Oh, to catch a butterfly!
What a delight it would be to a child!
But catching a butterfly would hurt its wings
And might cause him to die.
It's best not to see a butterfly die.
That is why butterflies are meant to be free and fly high!

Seeing a butterfly die
Is like seeing the death hidden under his lifeless, colorful wings.
When a butterfly is dead,
You see only the life in him
Because he is poised in a position that looks like he is resting on a
plant;
The tops of his wings are still vibrant with color and full of life.
It is only when the wind blows him away,
Which proves he cannot fly,

His wings frozen
And slightly open,
That you see his underside.
If you have ever seen the underside of a butterfly,
Then you have seen his death.
If you always look at his top side
And don't pay attention too closely
To how he rests,
Then you will never realize that he is dead.

In a way,
This is like never seeing death.
You are always seeing the life he has,
Not that he is dead.
And if you really think about it,
God helps him along.
With the gentle breeze that God sends by,
He carefully picks up the butterfly
And carries him away to rest,
And he is seen no more!
His death if not studied, is never seen or realized!
Then the earth remembers him no more,
And he is at peace, lovingly remembered by God.

Scripture Reference Based on Quoted Scripture the Poem Is Based On

Jesus said to her, "I am the resurrection and the life. He who believes in me will live, even though he dies; and whoever lives and believes in me will never die. Do you believe this?" (John 11:25–26 NIV) NIV One Touch Bible Soft Computer Program, 2019, www. biblesoft.com

How to See Abundant Life, Simply, Everywhere!

God's abundant life is all around us all of the time.
Oftentimes, so many people miss it.
They see it, but they do not perceive it.
Or perhaps they do not recognize it for what it is, and that is true life!

Abundant life can be simply seen in its most basic form: the beauty of God's creation all around us.
There is abundant life in God's creation all around us all of the time.
Most people miss this beauty because they are too busy with their complicated lives.

Take a minute the next time you want to see real life, and uncomplicate!
Then you will see abundant life!
Then you will truly be in awe of what God is capable of.
More than you can fathom?
Yes, it is!

When I see abundant life,
I see the miracle of the first winter's snow,
The joy it brings as it unites families and neighbors together to come and play and be happy.
The wonderful memories made by such a small gift God gives every season that brings us all together.

When I see abundant life,
I also see lush spring all around.

Green fields filled with flowers, grass, warm sunshine, happy birds singing, butterflies flying about.
I feel the freedom abundant life brings not only when I am in the wide-open, abandoned space of lush fields filled with sunshine and flowers,
But when this the spring's first cool afternoon shower washes down on me.

There is freedom hidden in abundant life, when you recognize it, and you are enjoying it, and you are happy, and you let go!
Then you are experiencing abundant life.
All it takes it for you to take a look around you and recognize God's handiwork.

Next time you experience abundant life,
Even if it is the first time,
Give thanks to Jesus Christ and to the Father Yahweh for creating and providing it for you,
To Yahweh for creating it.
And thank Jesus too,
For he is begotten of Yahweh,
Not made,
Of one being with Yahweh who is the Father.
Finally, know that Jesus Christ said that "I have come that you may have life, and have it to the full!"

Scripture Reference Based on Quoted Scripture Built around the Poem
The thief comes only to steal and kill and destroy; I have come that they may have life, and have it to the full. (John 10:10 NIV)
One Touch Bible Soft Computer Program, 2019, www.biblesoft.com

References

One Touch Bible Soft Computer Program, 2019, <u>www.biblesoft.com.</u>

$\mathcal{A}bout\ the\ \mathcal{A}uthor$

Amanda Libbers, May 21st 2020

I am a native of Baton Rouge, Louisiana. I attended and graduated from University Laboratory School (U-High), class of 1999; Southeastern Louisiana University, class of 2004; and Medical Training College, class of 2009. I attended the University of Louisiana at Monroe for one year (1999–2000) and Louisiana State University for one year (2000–2001), but I graduated from Southeastern Louisiana University in Hammond, Louisiana (2001–2004). I have a bachelor's of family and consumer science in the area of family studies from

Southeastern Louisiana University, and a diploma as a medical office specialist from Medical Training College. I held a national license to bill and code from January 2010 through January 2012 under the National Healthcare Association. I have not done much in my life since college because I lacked a clear direction to take. Finding what I am good at such as writing, has brought clear direction to my life more recently. I have always enjoyed writing a short story or poem whenever I get inspired. I have enjoyed writing this book because I always enjoy helping others and trying to make a difference in someone else's life! I believe that anyone is capable of making a difference in people's lives from day to day, no matter how small it is. Don't forget to ask yourself how you can help someone else in need today!

.

CPSIA information can be obtained
at www.ICGtesting.com
Printed in the USA
BVHW031055260620
582396BV00004B/36/J